THAT
PETER KAY
BOOK

THE STORY OF HOW PETER KAY BECAME
BOLTON'S BIGGEST EXPORT

Johnny Dee

D1322478

André Deutsch

To Kathy, Holly and Annie.
You are my sunshine.

Contents

'Imagination has given us the steam engine, the telephone, the talking-machine, and the automobile, for these things had to be dreamed of before they became realities. So I believe that dreams – daydreams, you know, with your eyes wide open and your brain machinery whizzing – are likely to lead to the betterment of the world. The imaginative child will become the imaginative man or woman most apt to invent, and therefore to foster, civilization.'

L. Frank Baum

'If you can talk with crowds and keep your virtue,
Or walk with kings – nor lose the common touch,
If neither foes nor loving friends can hurt you;
If all men count with you, but none too much,
If you can fill the unforgiving minute
With sixty seconds' worth of distance run,
Yours is the Earth and everything that's in it,
And – which is more – you'll be a Man, my son!'

Rudyard Kipling

'Garlic bread?'

Peter Kay

Introduction

It is 2 July 2002 and I am seated behind an enormous board table in a management office on Soho Square in the West End of London. I feel lonely. I haven't got an iPod or a newspaper to flick through and he's late. Outside, office workers are scattered around the small patch of grass in the middle of the square, motorcycle couriers dart in and out of traffic and I sit drumming my fingers waiting for him to arrive. I know he's in the building long before I see him – not because the building shakes as if he were King Kong or something, or because he's got a loud voice that bounces off the walls and makes you fall off your chair, but because I can hear people laughing. It's like a domino effect; a door opens somewhere in the building and a guffaw gushes out of it as if the room were filled with water. Then another person laughs, then another, I turn around and that's when I see him, perched on the edge of a secretary's desk holding an unfeasibly large chocolate birthday cake and asking her if she's all right, when she's going on her holidays, do her radiators need bleeding ... finally he enters the room, puts the cake down and asks, 'Do you want a brew?'

He's a big man, but not as big as he looks on TV. They say telly adds 10 pounds. In his case it's more like 20. And he looks younger, too, especially as I'm used to seeing him in a grey wig wearing a BHS cardigan and drinking from a vase. His skin is as soft as a baby's arse, but his handshake is as firm as a bricklayer's. He tells me it's his 29th birthday. Do I want some cake? Go on, you know you want to.

I am here to interview him for *The Guide*, a pocket-sized supplement of entertainment wonder that's slipped inside the *Guardian* every Saturday. Because the first episode of the new series he has just made features a few famous TV soundtracks scattered through it (*Van Der Valk, Black Beauty, Minder*) they have hit upon the idea of basing the article around his all-time favourite themes. But before we talk about those there's other stuff I want to know, standard stuff, like how old he was when he first decided he wanted to be a comedian (seven), what he did before, what his mum's like, but also questions about his new series and in particular the scene at the family fun day involving a giant inflatable penis. His answers are brilliant and funny and so long that I begin looking at the tape wheezing inside my dictaphone and worrying it's about to die. The problem is that in most interviews, as you listen to rock stars and actors answer, you're thinking, 'This is boring' or 'I won't be able to print this' or even 'Please say something funny'. But every word that comes out of the mouth of the man in front of me is comedy gold. It's ridiculous. I could fill up two whole issues of *The Guide* with this stuff but I've got only a couple of pages.

Eventually we move on to discussing old TV shows and every time I mention a programme he starts singing the theme tune word for word, and not just ones we all know, such as *Minder*, but obscure, forgotten ones such as *The Fall Guy* – 'I never spent much time in school/But I taught ladies plenty'. As if this wasn't impressive enough, at the merest mention of a programme title he will not only tell me what channel it was on, but what day of the week, the time and what was on before and after it. Pushed, he'd probably go through the adverts and continuity announcements too but instead he tells me about his life around the time of the show's being broadcast – about his grandad baby-sitting and his dad buying fish and chips every Friday and his mum tripping over with a mug of tea in the middle of *Flambards*.

After we've spent two hours together, with the birthday cake demolished, he chucks me his *Live at the Top of the Tower* video across the table and we say our goodbyes – ignorantly, I hadn't even known he had a stand-up act. It's only later when I watch it at home that night and nearly die from laughing so much that it fully dawns on me how lucky I've been. I'm too young ever to have met Stan Laurel or Eric Morecambe or Les Dawson or Ronnie Barker, but I've met the next in that line of British comedy legends. Ladies and gentlemen, Peter Kay.

Chapter One
It was Much Better in Rehearsal

'If you're born a Catholic, you're not born in hospital, you're born in guilt.'

Peter Kay

'When I was a kid I used to pray for a new bike. Then I realised that the Lord doesn't work that way, so I stole one and asked Him to forgive me ... and I got it!'

Emo Phillips

Peter John Kay was born on Monday, 2 July 1973. According to the local newspaper, the weather that day was typical of British summertime: sunny intervals and scattered showers. Whether or not it was that fine rain that soaks you right through is unspecified. The rest of the afternoon edition of the *Bolton Evening News* – then still a tablecloth-sized broadsheet – was awash with incident: platform shoes 'on way out', screamed a front-page headline, while elsewhere there was the scoop that a blonde beauty queen from Ramsbottom had come second in the Miss Cinema Europe contest and that Denis Law had signed for his old club, Manchester City. Meanwhile, in Little Hulton, a two-year-old toddler had survived a 15-foot fall from a bedroom window with just a small scratch on his head. On TV the highlight of the evening was *The Two Ronnies* on BBC2 at 9.25 p.m. with special guests Lynsey De Paul, Georgie Fame and Alan Price.

Two days after his son was born Michael Kay visited the *Bolton Evening News* offices and placed an announcement in the Births, Marriages and Deaths section: 'On July 2 1973 at Bolton District Hospital to Deirdre (née O'Neil) and Michael, a son (Peter), brother for Julie Ann. Thanks to all concerned.'

Michael – the son of a driller – and Deirdre (who was born Margaret but dropped it in favour of her middle name), the daughter of a cable layer, were married, both aged 20, at St Peter and Paul's Roman Catholic Church in Pilkington Street, Bolton, on 22 June 1968. Julie was born just over a year later. Back then Michael was a maintenance fitter in a cotton mill, but by the time Peter was impressing the teachers at St Ethelbert's Primary School with his Frank Spencer impressions (his first school report noted 'Peter seems unable to resist trying to amuse') he was working as an engineer at the Daubhill Ropeworks, while Deirdre had left her job as a chiseller at a paper mill to stay at home and raise the family – motherhood rather than chiselling being her calling.

When he was in his twenties and he was asked what his father did, Peter answered: 'I dunno, bash metal, that's what dads do, isn't it?'

The Kay family lived in Daubhill – Peter used to tell people, 'You say it like wobble except with D instead of W at the front' – with Michael's parents, Stanley and Edith. Daubhill was an area with a large south Asian community a mile or so from the town centre, which consisted mainly of two-up, two-down back-to-back houses that easily reinforce dated southern stereotypes of grim northern towns populated by women with headscarves over their rollers scrubbing their front steps. Shortly after Peter's birth Michael and Deirdre moved one street north, staying in the same area.

The streets where Peter Kay grew up seem pretty unchanged by the ravages of time, the occasional abandoned fridge freezer notwithstanding – indeed, judging by the sunlight-faded mutant ninja turtles toys in the window of Kola's on St Helens Road, many of the shops still have the same stock.

Peter's father was a small man, just over five feet tall, but, like most of the men employed by the ropeworks, he had an unquenchable thirst for alcohol. He'd spread his custom over half a dozen locals as well as the Ellesmere Road Social Club and would sink a few pints before moving on to the whisky, or later in his life, white wine. He was a funny man who deployed bone-dry sarcasm and enjoyed telling jokes, especially the punchlines, which he'd repeat mercilessly until everyone got them – 'Are you having that?' Peter's mother, who was born in Coalisland in County Tyrone, Northern Ireland, was, he says, very different, 'a bit mad, more laugh out loud'. Neighbours say the couple were 'like chalk and cheese'; Deirdre wasn't a drinker, so they were seldom seen out together.

Like many a good God-fearing Catholic tyke, Peter Kay was an altar boy from the age of five. 'Whenever he does an impression of a creepy priest,' says schoolfriend Karen Peel, whose brother was also an altar boy at St Ethelbert's Church in Deane at that time, 'I just know he's doing an impression of Father Flatley.'

Yet Father Flatley was a good man, too. In 1994 a baby was abandoned on his doorstep and he took the girl under his wing. At his funeral in December 2001, Peter said: 'He had a great understanding and helped a lot of people. I knew him well. It is very sad.'

As a child, however, Peter worshipped in front of a different altar from the one Father Flatley would have preferred: a 24-inch oblong one that took pride of place in the Kay living room. Aged eight, he saw a vision, his first celebrity in the flesh, when the family walked out to Four Lane Ends in nearby Farnworth one wet Sunday April morning and watched Jimmy Savile jog by in the Bolton Marathon. To commemorate the occasion Peter bought a novelty soap-on-a-rope *Jim'll Fix It* medal.

Fortunately Karen Peel, who went to the adjoining St Ethelbert's Roman Catholic Junior School, was around to witness Peter Kay's debut public performance in a production of *The Wizard of Oz* in the spring of 1984 to celebrate the 50th anniversary of the school. 'He was the Mayor of Munchkinland and I do remember him stealing the show a bit,' she recalls. 'He played a very good, middle-aged, portly mayor, which at the age of 11 was quite a thing to carry off.'

This wasn't to be the last occasion on which Peter would follow the yellow brick road. The next time, rather like Dorothy's trip over the rainbow, it would be an event that would change the course of his life for ever. Until then, though, there are 562 episodes of *Coronation Street* to sit through, not to mention a couple of series of *The Gentle Touch*, six years of *'Allo 'Allo*, Kevin Keegan falling off his bike in *Superstars*, Five Star being called wankers in a phone-in on *Going Live*, and two rubber balls telling jokes in Irish accents on *Why Don't You?*. Then there's a lifetime of *Take Hart* with Tony Hart, *Top Cat*, *The Professionals*, *Loveboat*, *Dallas* and a couple of hundred chances for couples to win Bully's special prize on *Bullseye*.

> I can't go away with you on a rock climbing weekend,
> What if something's on TV and it's never shown again?
> *The Lemonheads*, 'The Outdoor Type'

TV was not just an addiction for the young Peter Kay; it was much, much more than that. In 2001, when he appeared in the *I Love the 1970s* series of nostalgia shows, friends told him he must have been sent clips of the shows he commented on because he'd only have been a toddler when they were on.

'I wasn't, honest, people think I'm lying,' he says. 'In 1976 I was three but I remember what was on telly.

'Television was so much a part of my life, I loved it,' he told me. 'A lot of my friends were out playing football and things like that, but TV was like a religion for me. You had to be in front of the telly when a programme started or you missed it.'

Where other kids' lives would be measured out by football fixtures or exams, Peter Kay's ran to the timetable supplied by the *Radio Times*.

'*Minder* always reminds me of Wednesday nights at nine o clock,' he says. 'Benny Hill would be on at eight. I'd go to bed at 8.30 and I'd always hear the *Minder* theme tune through the floor: "If you want to I'll change the situation ...". Then I'd hear the front door close and my dad going out and I knew where he'd be going; he'd send us to bed and then go and get fish and chips. He'd come back and I'd always come down and go, "I can't sleep ... ooooh fish and chips" ... and he'd go, "Ah, all right, you can have a butty." So I'd stay and watch a bit of *Minder*.'

Saturdays meant *The Pink Panther Show*, *Dr Who*, *Jim'll Fix It*, *3-2-1* and his dad's night to cook.

'We'd have breakfast at night-time, because it was all he knew how to make, so we'd have full English for tea.'

Peter's fear of missing something life-changing on TV abated in the early 1980s, when the Kays were among the first families on Willows Lane to buy a video recorder – a Ferguson Videostar top loader with a remote control on a lead. According to family legend, when Peter would press rewind on this primitive piece of hi-tech the whole house would shake. Soon Peter was matching his sister's obsession with filling a C-90 with the Top 40 chart rundown minus the 'this is Mike Read on 275 and 285' bits with an ambitious plan to videotape virtually everything. Soon his bedroom would be lined with entire runs of *'Allo 'Allo*, *Porridge* and his favourite in his early teenage years, a sit-com starring an alien from the planet Ork who once laid a giant egg from which his son emerged and enjoyed something of a romantic liaison with a puzzled young lady from Boulder, Colorado.

'I've got every episode of *Mork and Mindy* on video except the last one,' he says. 'There were ninety-five. The last f***ing episode of *Mork and Mindy*! I taped it religiously, because when I was a kid I loved it. I started taping them thinking there won't be that many ... I've got *Mork and Mindy* Volume 8, Volume 9 ... Every Wednesday I'd run home from school and tape them religiously. I carried on and I went to Spain in 1991 and it was the last episode of *Mork and Mindy* and I sent cards from Spain, I rang up from Spain saying, "Tape it, tape it." Did they tape it? Did they f***! It was on recently and the theme came on and I had this rush of being a child and my dad laughing so much at it.'

Peter's elder sister Julie also made full use of the new technology in the house and would hold regular Saturday movie afternoons for her pals where, unbeknown to Deirdre Kay, they'd watch 'video nasties' such as *Driller Killer* and *I Spit on Your Grave*. 'Mum'd be knocking on door going, "Your dinner's ready, are you coming or what?"' says Peter.

In years to come, of course, the Ferguson Videostar would feature in Peter's stand-up act when he recalled how his father would put a cushion over it whenever they left the house to prevent it being stolen. 'Nobody'd steal it,' jokes Peter. 'It were too bloody heavy.'

The video recorder also came in handy when, aged 13, he broke his ankle and spent a fortnight off school. With his son having to spend the entire time at home on the sofa, Michael Kay struck a cut-price deal with the local video shop – Take Two – if he agreed to hire two films a day. And so began Kay's love of films and, in particular, camp sci-fi musical *Flash Gordon*, which in turn led to an obsession with the band who had provided the soundtrack, Queen. Surprisingly, when you consider how often he is compared with Les Dawson and Eric Morecambe, the first comedians Peter Kay loved were Americans: Robin Williams (who starred as Mork), Steve Martin and master of the deadpan one-liner Steven Wright. His favourite movies were American too: Mel Brooks's *Blazing Saddles* and *The Producers* and the Zucker Brothers' brilliant parody of airborne disaster movies, *Airplane!*. He bought the stand-up records like Steven Wright's *I Have a Pony*, and soundtrack albums of all of them, and he would spend hours taping them and splicing them between strange vinyl oddities he found at the record store on Bolton Market and at Manchester discount stores, compiling what he called 'Crap Trax' on to cassette tapes for the amusement of his friends.

'They were brilliant,' remembers schoolfriend Michael Atherton. 'They'd have songs from Manhattan Transfer, Telly Savalas – Peter had all his albums and even wrote him a fan letter. There'd be "Theme from *Love, American Style*", John Inman from *Are You being Served* with a military brass band, I shit you not, Patrick Macnee and "Kinky Boots". Every track would be interspersed with blipvert clips from *Airplane!* like "Joey, have you ever been in a Turkish prison?" and various other things. I was really jealous of Peter's record collection.'

Mount St Joseph's in Hawthorne Road, Deane, opened in 1902 and was the first Roman Catholic secondary school in England to be built under the Balfour Education Act. Until 1979 it was a girls' grammar school, but in 1979 it became a co-educational secondary school. The school buildings were tagged on to a crumbling old convent, home to the authoritarian headmistress, Sister Barbara.

'She didn't like Peter,' remembers Karen Peel. 'But then I

don't think she liked me either. I don't think she liked children, full stop. She was an archetypal, stuck-up, prudish Irish nun. She didn't like the idea of working-class boys spoiling her school.'

'I don't think she ever got over the school switching from all girls,' says Michael Atherton.

Despite the ominous presence of the nuns, Mount St Joseph's wasn't what might be described today as a centre of excellence. But what it lacked in academic prowess it made up for in other ways. Peter joined in with all the school holiday trips, to Wales and, most memorably, in 1987 to the tiny nature reserve, the Isle of Rhum in the Inner Hebrides of Scotland, the population of which doubled with the visit of 30-odd schoolkids from Bolton. Before the trip Peter told his father he needed a proper coat, because they were going walking and climbing. But Kay Senior's idea of what constituted a proper coat for a school trip differed somewhat from his son's and he returned from town with a luminous yellow jacket Peter described as the kind of thing people wear when they're working on motorways. Embarrassed by his garish jacket though he was, one day on the holiday it came in handy when they explored the rugged Cuillin Mountains, where they would be staying overnight in a remote and very basic hostel building. For safety's sake the Mount St Joseph kids were split into two, but then, disastrously, one of the groups went missing.

'It was very emotional; they were missing for about four hours, but it turned out they'd just gone down the wrong side of the mountain and had to trek all the way round,' remembers Karen Peel. 'When they turned up there were hugs and kisses. We thought they'd died.'

Peter Kay loved talking about this dramatic calamity and in particular about the ferryman who appeared out of the mist with a raised lantern like something out of John

Carpenter's *The Fog*, shouting 'Is everyone all right?', which ironically petrified half the schoolkids he was supposed to be rescuing.

'You'd never get away with school trips like that now, I suppose,' muses Karen Peel. 'We even had non-official trips organised by the teachers that had nothing to do with the school. Mount St Joseph's was quite old-fashioned in that it saw itself as part of the community,' she says. 'It had that family, community spirit thing where it didn't feel like you were at school sometimes. There was always some sort of club going on after school, dancing, drama or art, and Peter would always be there.'

Peter was a paper boy for Chris's News, a newsagent on his street, Willows Lane, from the age of 11 to 16 and was popular with both the old-age pensioners on his route (for whom he'd regularly do odd bits of shopping) and the small kids (one summer, he bought a whole box of giant ice pops from the shop and distributed them among the children on his round). After delivering the *Bolton Evening News* every afternoon he would rush back to Mount St Joseph's.

In the winter term of 1985, Peter's first year at the school, inspired by Band Aid, teacher Paul Abbott wrote a tune called 'Song for the Starving' and had 6,000 copies pressed on vinyl. During the recording Abbott scolded Peter for changing the lyrics and making the other singers laugh. 'Life's just a joke to you, Kay. Life's a joke,' he yelled. The line stayed with Peter throughout his school life and almost became his first catchphrase, as he would mockingly repeat it to himself behind the teachers' backs.

Peter also featured in a fashion show for CAFOD and in the annual talent contest held each year on St Joseph's Day, where he would sing or tell a few jokes. The majority of the school saw such activities as spectacularly uncool; not that this bothered Peter who, uncooler still, counted some of the staff among his friends, particularly art teacher John Clough.

'Him and John Clough were like two peas in a pod,' remembers Karen Peel. 'You'd walk into the room and they'd be chuckling about something. I'm sure he had a big influence on Peter's humour. He was a great bloke, not like a teacher at all really, he used to bring in cake.' Clough, whom Peter described as being 'the spitting image of Gorden Kaye in *'Allo 'Allo*' and 'really laid-back', also influenced his star pupil's music taste, making him cassettes of crusty rock artists such as Genesis and Dan Fogelberg. For someone who had grown up in a house with just five albums (*The Best of the Carpenters, The Best of the Beach Boys, The Best of Simon & Garfunkel, The Best of Tony Christie* and 'something Irish') it was a revelation. 'He showed films in art lessons and he used to get us to draw lyrics of Beatles songs,' remembers Peter. 'He made me see that art was not just in pictures in a frame, but also in film and cinematography – all around us. He made a big impression on my life.'

'Peter had this abstract way of seeing things,' John Clough, who still teaches at Mount St Joseph's, says. 'Even though he wouldn't really answer the question, he would say something even more interesting. Of course he was very popular with his classmates, being such an entertainer. But he was also a strangely calming influence.'

Kay's calming influence extended beyond the classroom into the playground. According to Michael Atherton there were some rough kids at the school, but they didn't spend long on Peter. 'He had a way of disarming people,' he recalls. 'But at the same time he'd be taking the piss out of them. He wasn't all that overweight at the time. Peter was picked on a bit, as was I for that matter, for being slightly filled out, which probably counted as fat to the street-hardened wastrels doing the picking.'

'I was bullied a bit, but it was only mild, nothing major,' remembers Peter himself. 'They called me fat and I'd just make a joke of it and say, "Yeah, I am, aren't I?" It was my own fault, I ate too much.'

'I just think most kids didn't know how to take him,' says Karen Peel. 'Most kids gave him a look of "I don't know what you're on about, you're just that strange kid who's a bit funny but I don't know why you're funny because I don't understand you". I used to hang out with Peter and Catherine, Michael and the Smith twins, Jane and Claire. He didn't really seem to have many male friends. He wasn't into football, he wasn't into the stuff average teenage boys were into; he was more interested in messing about with videos.'

Interviewed recently, Patrick McGuinness, who would be given his big acting break by Peter as a lecherous bouncer, pointed up the difference between himself and his friend: 'At school, although we were mates, we had different interests really. Peter was into sitting in his bedroom and listening to the words off songs and then writing them down, or taping stuff off the telly. I was just interested in getting my end away!'

It wasn't just his friends or John Clough's cake and Genesis albums that attracted Peter back into school when he could have been at home watching *Rentaghost*. There was the art and music lab which, as well as all the standard school paraphernalia, contained video editing equipment and a hand-held video camera. By virtue of the fact that he was the only person in the school who knew how to use it all, he became the school's unofficial cameraman. When nuns and priests from across Europe visited the school for Caring Church Week he was given the task, by Sister Barbara, of documenting the occasion. The nuns were happy with the results, but didn't know he'd made another copy, over which he'd dubbed the nuns and priests telling jokes. He was also using the equipment for video versions of his 'Crap Trax', to which he'd give titles like *Weasels* and copy for Michael Atherton and John Clough.

'Mentally scarred by football', he did have one hobby that took place outside the school gates. With two of his classmates (Warren Powell and Paul Coleman) he formed something of a comedy troupe cum prototype *Jackass*. Originally calling themselves the All Stars, they later became known as the Tree-ers (after the Irish pronunciation of the number three). The main *modus operandi* of this primi-tive comedy gang was to steal the school's video camera and take it into Bolton town centre, where they would film their skits: surfing shopping trolleys in Morrison's car park and re-creating the opening titles of *Dallas* on the corner of Trinity Street, outside Comet. The best idea of all, though, was interviewing old-age pensioners, bombarding them with a series of baffling, incoherent questions in order to film their puzzled reactions. In one compilation, 'They Flew by Night', Peter can be heard chuckling behind the camera while he asks a greying old biddy 'Whaddya-think-of-the-time-o-life-the-kinda-know?' and 'Is it prison of life?'

For comedy historians this tape alone would be evidence enough that Peter Kay was always destined for greatness. But there is another video, wobbly and out of focus though it is, that records the moment he became a star in waiting.

Somewhere over the rainbow
Skies are blue,
And the dreams that you dare to dream
Really do come true.

E. Y. Harburg, 'Somewhere Over the Rainbow'

Another of Peter Kay's duties was performing as the school DJ, although as Karen Peel is keen to stress, it 'was silly DJ-ing, not proper DJ-ing'.

'Let's just say he were no Judge Jules,' says another friend, Sonia Hurst, who witnessed Kay and his DJ partner in crime Michael Atherton on their hired wheels of steel together with flashing traffic light special effects. Pupils would bring in their records to be played at the irregular Friday-night events, scrawling their names on the sleeves, but Peter would sabotage the proceedings by splicing in the occasional piece of comedy dialogue from Leonard Rossiter in *Rising Damp*, Peter Cook and Dudley Moore's Derek and Clive comedy albums, Steve Martin's 'Grandpa bought a rubber' joke. Karen Peel also remembers Kay grabbing the microphone and impersonating the cheesy vocal stylings of a mobile DJ, interspersing songs with cries of 'shabba' and 'this one's for the laydeez'. Throughout, Sister Barbara would be prowling the floor to make sure there was no 'funny business'.

Peter would spend hours at home with his knackered double-deck ghetto blaster assembling the tapes he'd use to insert classic comedy TV moments between the hits of the day. He'd also include choice sections from the first record he ever purchased – a BBC Library sound effects album – speeding cars, canned laughter and explosions.

Even after he left school, Peter Kay still had a hand in the Friday-night discos, handing Michael Atherton, who was in the year below him, tapes together with long written-out lists as to when to insert the necessary between-song gag or clip. Michael kept two sheets of instructions for a fifth-form leavers' disco on 25 May 1990. Among the soundbite clips Peter Kay had assembled for his friend was Jimmy Cagney's classic 'Top of the world, Ma' line from *White Heat*, the *A Team* theme tune, a Radio One jingle and 'The Birdy Song'. Kay also included various snippets from James H. Reeves's late-night phone-in show, 'Nocturnal Emissions', on Manchester's Radio Piccadilly. Reeves was notorious for getting the sack from the station in 1981 for playing the

Queen song 'Killer Queen' after a news item about a 17-year-old student shooting blank bullets at the monarch during Trooping of the Colour. In the late 1980s Reeves played host to an expanding list of Mancunian eccentrics who would ring and share jokes such as 'Did you hear about that artist fellow with the dirty finger on one hand? That's right, he was called Picasso.' Among Reeves's own favourite japes was to read out car registration numbers of bad drivers and to attack mundane areas of British society such as the post office, government forms and Christmas TV. A cassette of these monologues, *Pocket Emissions*, was Peter's most cherished possession aged 13 as well as his own tapes of Reeves's 'Worst Records of the Year' show.

After they left school Peter and Michael earned some extra cash by DJ-ing at parties and even family weddings – all employing their trusted music and comedy cut-and-paste technique. 'Hi Ho Silver Lining' was followed by a James H. Reeves rant, 'Come On Eileen' with a sound effect of a horse clopping up a street.

'I do think the people at the weddings thought it was a bit odd,' says Michael. 'We were playing to a minority audience, really. It made us laugh.'

Peter, though, took the DJ-ing seriously and still counts among his proudest achievements keeping a wedding reception crowd in Clitheroe dancing for two solid hours. According to Catherine Hurst, who became Peter's first girlfriend when she asked him out at the age of 14, 'He always thought he'd end up being a wedding DJ.'

As well as being his girlfriend, Catherine – who had a dry, laid-back sense of humour – was also his comedy foil and when they were out the pair would often slip into character and start repeating lines from *Airplane!*. As a schoolboy Michael Atherton remembers that his friend was 'always on' and looking for comedy in everything – impersonating the teachers' vocal tics and movements. Whenever anyone mentioned the name of the metalwork teacher Mr Callan, Peter would stand up and mime swinging a light bulb like the scene in the title sequence of the *Callan* TV thriller series starring Edward Woodward. He'd also hear double meanings in the things people would say, where others might miss them. Once in the dining room somebody commented that the dried-out chips 'aren't that clever', to which Kay responded, 'What, chips trying to do algebra on the plate?' When anyone would ask 'Who's farted?' he would pantomime opening a giant ledger containing details of everyone who'd ever farted in the history of mankind.

'He'd also plant mental seeds in his audience to pay off on later, much as he and other stand-ups do today,' claims Michael Atherton. 'He suggested to everyone that a school roller blind featured a massive picture of [*North West Tonight* and *It's a Knockout* presenter] Stuart Hall. Consequently every time the teacher went to unfurl the blind Pavlovian sniggers of anticipation would be heard from the back.'

But despite his obvious intelligence, lessons held little interest for Peter Kay. 'He was always in the bottom class, but he'd doctor his reports before his mum saw them,' says Catherine Hurst. 'He was like you see him on telly, he never took anything seriously. He wasn't shy at all. He was very romantic; for my 16th birthday he bought me 16 presents and made me a tape with songs that had 16 in the title.'

It's true that Peter never shone academically – he once got 3 per cent in a maths exam – but through after-school activities he gained the self-confidence he didn't get from learning about ancient Greeks or logarithms. There was also his sense of humour. Karen Peel remembers that it went over the top of most people's heads: 'This was the 1980s and although his kind of observational humour is common now, back then people didn't get it half the time.'

Peter was very much the class clown but, more than this, he was, in the words of Michael Atherton, 'someone who was only comfortable as the centre of attention'. If his humour wasn't recognised by some of his schoolmates or the nuns (who Peter says were 'in and out of school like the hokey cokey'), at least some of the teachers got it. Art teacher John Clough recalls that he had a 'mischievous creativity'. 'He always had it,' he says, 'that natural funniness, but he wasn't sure how to channel it.'

That moment arrived when, after much nagging, he landed the part of the Cowardly Lion in the Mount St Joseph's production of *The Wizard of Oz*. This was a much bigger affair than the one at St Ethelbert's when he'd shone as the Mayor of Munchkinland. Far from being a small event, the musical was chosen as the moment to mark the end of the school's history on the current site – just a few weeks later the old school and convent was to be demolished, and when the new term year began pupils would switch to the new school in Greenland Road, Farnworth.

'We didn't do much drama at school,' remembers Peter. 'We'd do little plays in class, where we would all read out parts, but if you ever did it in a different voice, everyone would laugh hysterically – "What are you doing? Don't do a voice!" When I got the part of the Lion, teachers said it would be difficult with my exams coming up. Then I did fail most of my exams! I always just loved making people laugh. That's what I did. I was never an idiot. I was never brilliantly academic, I just wanted to make people laugh. When it got to exam time I just thought, "I don't know if I can be bothered."'

The Wizard Of Oz, felt the headmistress Sister Barbara, was all about new beginnings, and the new school site was to be their gleaming educational version of L. Frank Baum's Emerald City. *The Wizard of Oz* was also good, clean, wholesome family fun. For four nights from Wednesday, 19 April 1989 to Saturday, 22 April 1989 the school gym was taken over and various dignitaries – the local bishop, Father Flatley and the mayor of Bolton – were invited. The school art department spent months putting together an elaborate stage set to match the one Judy Garland journeyed across, while Mrs Jasmik, the head of needlework ('It was that kind of school!' says Michael), toiled away on the costumes. Peter's orangey fake fur lion suit will be familiar to anyone who's watched his career closely – its most recent appearance was in the 2005 Comic Relief video for '(Is This the Way to) Amarillo', in which he wore it flanked by Danny Baker as a scarecrow and Heather 'Mrs Paul McCartney' Mills as Dorothy, but he also wore it for his *Live at the Top of the Tower* video and it's also made fleeting appearances on various TV shows through the years. Decidedly less weather-worn than it is now, on the nights of *The Wizard of Oz* show it was topped off with face paint, a yellow smock top and Bermuda shorts with the words 'Grrr', 'Roar' and 'Growl' written across them in permanent marker. In a touch that was completely Peter's own the ensemble was topped off with a pair of Ray Ban sunglasses.

'The show was a really big deal,' remembers Karen Peel, who had the role of the Scarecrow. 'Sister Barbara was clucking around backstage. When the bishop came we were told that had to be the best night and to be sensible. Then on the final night we were told, "You've done a really good job, have fun, just relax, enjoy yourselves", which Peter took as his cue. We were all giddy anyway.'

Having studied Bert Lahr's performance, and particularly his southern drawl, in the 1939 musical, Peter Kay delivered his lines in a Texas accent that occasionally slipped into deepest Boltonian – the resulting scramble ended up sounding like Eric Morecambe in one of Ernie Wise's 'plays wot I wrote'. This alone was enough to have the audience in stitches, but there was more: Peter was virtually in a play on his own, ad-libbing and slipping out of character. 'That's not even a funny line,' he tells the audience who are laughing at his character's sincere fear of travelling to Oz to find some courage; 'it was much better in rehearsal.' Incredibly, he says all this deadpan and without cracking a smile or giggling at his nerve.

'When he was supposed to be onstage he'd be up and down the aisle swinging his tail or shouting "Hello mums",' remembers Karen Peel. 'He'd go and sit on people's laps or pull faces. At one point I could have crucified him because I was supposed to be dancing with him onstage and he just buggered off.'

This was during the jitterbug scene when Dorothy, the Lion, Scarecrow and Tin Man decide that the answer to their problems is to travel to see the all-knowing Grand Pooh-Bah of Oz in his impressive palace. But leaving his co-stars mid-jitterbug, Peter decided to go completely off script and do a solo wiggle to the back of the stage, where he cocked his leg and pretended to pee up against a tree (actually, in the grand tradition of British school plays where everyone gets a part, the tree was really a small girl from the second year). 'It was just complete, absolute chaos,' says Karen Peel. 'In the interval Sister Barbara grabbed hold of us backstage and gave us this massive lecture, saying she expected more of us, that the mayor was in the audience and we were letting the school down. We just ignored her and continued along similar lines. Peter wouldn't have paid any attention anyway; it was all water off a duck's back to him. No one took her very seriously.'

Sister Barbara should possibly have expected Peter's grandstanding, considering the fact that a few years earlier in the nativity, playing the innkeeper, he'd offered Mary and Joseph 'an en-suite with full English'.

The school video camera, set up on a tripod by Peter, captured all four performances of *The Wizard of Oz* and, in an early example of his meticulousness, he spent hours editing the best parts of all four of his performances for the final videotape which was copied for the cast. The tape also showed off his now customary cut-and-pasting skills, with a big-band version of '(Is This the Way to) Amarillo' and audience clapping from a sound effects album shoehorned on to the front and the final credits from *The Wizard of Oz* movie tacked on to the end.

Although time and technology haven't been kind to the copy of the video Karen Peel keeps tucked away at the back of a cupboard, it provides a brilliant insight into the young Peter Kay. The first thing that strikes you is that he's funny without even trying; just the sight of him makes the audience laugh. Despite everyone describing him as a fat kid, he wasn't all that overweight, but even then at age 15 he has the look of a middle-aged man – specifically Alf Roberts from *Coronation Street* – trapped inside a child's body.

The final five minutes of the *The Wizard of Oz* tape is taken up with another Peter Kay project. After school one warm sunny day, just weeks before it was due to be demolished, he filmed a tour of the school with a video camera mounted on a skateboard. There are also artistic pans of wire fences, the dinner hall and the school tuck shop, and in one flash of humour Kay himself dancing with a dinner lady while he smiles and winks hammily at the camera. Peter set the film to a soundtrack of Phil Collins's 'Take Me Home' from the *No Jacket Required* album and presented it to John Clough as a parting gift.

'I loved school so much that when I left I had a hard time really getting over it,' Peter reveals today. 'The problem was we left on the Friday and on the Saturday the bulldozers

came in and demolished the school – it became a car park.'
But Peter was lucky – the pupils at the relocated school not
only mourned the loss of their old home, but also had to put
up with the new one being treated like a brand-new sofa with
the cellophane left on by the nuns. Every day they had to take
two different pairs of shoes to school (indoor and outdoor).

Unlike many kids, who can't wait to leave school, Peter
Kay dreaded it – as is borne out by his sentimental video for
John Clough. 'He never used to talk about his home life,' says
Karen Peel. 'Never mentioned his mum or his dad. I always
thought he was a bit of a loner and I think a lot of the reason
he used to hang around at school with the likes of John
Clough was that he didn't want to go home.' In fact his home
life was a happy one. At home he'd run errands for his nan,
his father's mother Edith, who lived in their old house at 71
Croston Street. And between bouts of TV watching there
would be family weddings, birthdays, trips to Northern
Ireland and holidays to Wales, Butlin's in Minehead and a
Warner's holiday camp in Burnham on Sea where Peter and
his mum went to see Nik Kershaw perform live.

'And we'd go to Blackpool about six times a year,' he says.
'My mum would go, "I fancy a change. I know, let's go to
Blackpool." It mentally scarred me, especially the B&B we
stayed in; my dad got a 10 per cent discount at this really
rough place that had a sign up near the door that said
"Arrive as guests, leave as friends".'

As with much of Peter's life, the stories about Blackpool
and his dad would be re-created in the future. 'They're all
true,' he says. 'My dad really was obsessed with getting up
early to make the most of the holiday. He'd leap out of bed
at 6 a.m., go for a walk on the front, buy a newspaper and
come back and insist on everyone getting up. We'd be going,
"Ah, Dad, come on, it's only half past seven; we're on
holiday." '

But trouble was brewing between his parents, and by the time Peter left Mount St Joseph's they had separated. The cause was his father's drinking, made worse by the fact that he had been forced into early retirement from the ropeworks with osteoporosis, a bone disease that can be brought on by alcoholism and hard manual labour. Michael's condition had one important effect on his son: he never went near a drop of alcohol. 'Because we were never the type of Bolton teenager who hangs around outside the offy drinking Thunderbird Peter being teetotal was never really an issue,' says Michael Atherton. 'Seeing his father the worse for drink most nights probably had something to do with it.' According to Catherine Hurst, Peter 'used to tell people he had an illness because he got fed up with people asking him why he didn't drink'.

At 16, with his father gone and his sister Julie living with her new husband, Kay found himself the chief breadwinner in the house following his parents' divorce, writing letters for his mother looking for new housing saying, 'I am a divorced mother of two seeking sheltered accommodation.' Instead, Peter and Deirdre moved back to 71 Croston Street while his grandad and nan moved out to a warden-controlled house a few streets away. Peter joked to Michael Atherton that it was particularly noisy in their house on Saturday mornings, a reference to the Sandi Toksvig-fronted kids' TV show *No. 73*.

In typical style Peter remembers the moment his mother and father announced their separation to him – it was halfway through an episode of *Mork and Mindy*. While it might be tempting to imagine Peter Kay was scarred by these events and that it shaped his comedy, it isn't the case. 'It's true he never talked much about his dad's problems or parents' divorce,' says Michael Atherton today. 'But then again we were a bunch of teenage lads, not the cast of *Thirtysomething*.' Pressed on the matter, Peter Kay will tell you that his parents' divorce was amicable. 'It wasn't that bad really,' he has said, adamant that there'll be 'none of that tears of a clown bollocks from me'.

His father went to live with another woman, Margaret Faulkner, and father and son saw each other regularly every weekend. If you are looking to find some misery behind the mirth of Peter Kay, then it is not here.

In August 1989, Michael Atherton arranged a week-long 'end of an era' holiday in his parents' caravan in the Lake District, inviting Peter and Catherine, Karen Peel, the Smith twins as well as teachers John Clough and Gerald Greathead, who taught history. 'I know that seems a little bizarre in hindsight but it seemed quite normal at the time,' laughs Michael Atherton. 'I know it's not the norm and people who went to other schools probably think it's a bit weird, but those teachers were like mates,' says Karen. 'Some people stayed in the caravan, some people camped, and we just had a farewell good laugh basically. We'd all been a bit of a gang, and after that Claire and Jane were going off to college in Wigan; it felt like the end of something.'

At the time Peter enjoyed giving complex things names – such as his beloved Leonard Maltin's *Movie Almanac*, which he called 'Bob' – and promptly dubbed the holiday 'Gareth'. Still high on his *Wizard of Oz* success, Peter and Michael used the holiday to impress the gang with their thespian skills and spent much of their time acting out a bleak improvised Harold Pinteresque play when pressed to do the washing up or fetch a Calor gas bottle.

'Go.'

'I'm going.'

'Go then.'

'Yes.'

'I'm gone.'

'I guess you had to be there,' chuckles Michael Atherton,

who soon afterwards dropped his acting aspirations and became a website designer. 'Peter was always funny. The problem was how to make a living out of it.'

If he'd been born to middle-class parents in west London rather than a working-class family from Lancashire, Peter Kay would no doubt have been directed to the nearest drama school, where he'd have ended up starring in *Grange Hill* or being cajoled on to the West End stage as one of Fagin's pickpocketing gang. Instead, it was the not so bright lights of the Bolton College on Manchester Road and, thinking that acting was his future, a BTEC in Performing Arts. At the interview he told the tutor simply, 'I'm a funny person.' It wasn't a happy time. 'It was a bit hard,' he says, looking back. 'It was the first year they'd done it. We started off as 20 and at the end there was just three of us. I really went off the thought of acting or doing drama after I left there in 1991; I more or less decided that being creative wasn't for me. I was really despondent after that.'

Adding to his unhappiness was the death of his grandad, to whom he was very close.

'His grandad was a source of comedy inspiration, too,' says Michael Atherton. 'He was forever shouting "Rub-yed!", a somewhat inexplicable cry related to rubbing your head.' This was a sad time for Peter, but as Michael Atherton explains, even in his darkest time he was still looking for comedy. 'There were times when the laughter stopped,' says Michael. 'There were times when Peter was quick to anger, or hard on people. But aren't we all like that at times? The notable thing was that he always managed to eventually find some levity in the situation, and I think use that to work through the hard times, such as his parents' divorce or his grandad's death.'

Despite thoughts of forgetting all ideas about a future in entertainment and harbouring reservations about acting,

Peter continued to keep his hand in by joining the Bolton
Octagon Youth Theatre and working in the box office. The
Octagon job was one of many part-time positions Peter Kay
would hold between 1990 and 1998. With his father and
sister no longer at home, he needed them to help out there,
but he hated every single one of them. The jobs, however,
gave him something that no Performing Arts course ever
could: material.

Chapter Two

Eye Level is Buy Level

'The trouble with the rat race is that even if you win, you're still a rat.'

Lily Tomlin

'He who laughs most, learns best.'

John Cleese

In 1990, aged 17, Marc Rowlands, an A-level student who would later go on to be a journalist for Manchester listings magazine *City Life* and later the *Guardian*, went to a party at his friend Marcus Hulme's house. Marcus was taking advantage of his parents being away on a caravanning holiday to throw open his doors for the youth of Bolton.

'A few of us were sat upstairs listening to Massive Attack's *Blue Lines*, drinking booze we were too young for, when a lad came in, crying with laughter,' Rowlands remembers. 'He insisted that we follow him back downstairs and there, in the front room, was this stocky kid with a really broad Bolton accent entertaining 20 or so people with these stories about his job and his mum and dad. He was hysterical. That was the first time I met him.'

After this Marc would often run into Peter Kay at parties around town. He would always see him around 2 a.m. – the only sober person there – with a huge crowd of kids around him, just laughing their heads off. 'Peter was a popular lad, really well liked; people had heard of him all over Bolton. It's mad, I know, but the things he was saying weren't all that different to the stuff that made it into his stand-up show years later,' says Marc. 'For example, I remember him doing impressions of his mum with an Irish accent and about her buying shit cola from the Spar when he really wanted Coke. A lot of his stuff was a bit more blue than he'd do today, though.'

Kay also had another party trick up his sleeve. For years he'd been filling an E-180 videotape with the opening titles of his favourite and not so favourite TV shows – just the opening titles, relentlessly, one after the other – everything from crime shows such as *The Professionals* to the long-forgotten drama set on board a North Sea ferry, *Triangle*. 'You probably think that's sad, don't you?' he asked me in 2002. 'But when you put that tape on at two in the morning, when everyone's pissed, people love it.'

As well as the opening titles tape he had another with just adverts and even one dedicated to closedowns – hard to imagine now but TV stations didn't broadcast for 24 hours until the era of Sky and home shopping. ' "That's it from Granada. Whatever you're doing tonight don't forget to have a nice night," ' he says, imitating the continuity announcers of his youth. ' "Don't forget, your local radio stations are still on air and don't forget to unplug your set from the wall." And then the screen would turn black or they'd play the National Anthem. What were you supposed to do? Stand to attention? Sing along? And then there'd be a zzzzzzz and you had to wake up in case you got some brain thing.'

Missing school and his role as class clown, the teenage Peter Kay found a new outlet for his humour when in the summer of 1990 he took a part-time job working the 6-to-10 p.m. shift at the Majestic Garage, an Esso petrol station on St Helens Road, the main road between Daubhill and Bolton town centre. The best thing about it was that his friends were allowed to hang out there with him as he worked the till and, thanks to the management's liberal attitude to stocktaking, could eat as many packets of crisps and drink as much free pop (and not that Rola Cola either, proper stuff like Lilt) as they wanted.

'We were his audience, basically,' says Michael Atherton who, along with Marc Rowlands – whose friend Marcus Hulme also had a shift at the garage – and a few other ex-Mount St Joseph lads, would spend their evenings at the Majestic. 'From the minute somebody would arrive on the forecourt he'd do this running commentary on them for the benefit of his mates in the shop with him,' remembers Marc Rowlands. 'By the time they got to the door of the shop he'd told their whole life story, and the customers couldn't understand why the moment they walked through the door they'd be faced with these kids hiding behind the counter giggling into their hands.'

Among his other favourite things to do at the garage was abusing his access to the Tannoy system by yelling 'boo' to scare people innocently filling up their Ford Fiestas with £10 of unleaded or announcing non-existent special offers to an empty forecourt. He also particularly enjoyed visits from the feral kids from the nearby estate whose missions to steal Twixes and Yorkie bars he would thwart by adopting the mannerisms of a 1950s shopkeeper, roughing up their hair and playfully yanking at their cheeks until they'd disappear out of sheer embarrassment. Another one of his pastimes, remembers Michael Atherton, was to wave off customers with DJ catchphrases: ' "Don't go changing", he'd tell them as they left the shop, or "Keep your feet on the ground and keep reaching for the stars".'

The garage was also the venue for one of Peter's first comic creations: Derek Bollock, a twisted, bitter character who'd threaten to put children on a spike, 'and I don't mean Jeffrey Holland in *Hi-De-Hi*', if they dared cross him.

As well as his friends, there was another visitor to the Majestic Garage who would have a far-reaching effect on Kay's comedy synapses. He was an eccentric gentleman in his early fifties who, according to Michael Atherton, looked like a cross between 'Martin Jarvis and Derek Jacobi with a voice approaching Duncan Norvelle'. (Norvelle, in case you have forgotten, was a comic of the old-school pre-alternative comedy era whose catchphrase was camply to witter 'Oooh chase me, chase me'. This type of thing was strangely popular in the early 1980s, and Norvelle was a regular on ITV game shows such as *Celebrity Squares* and *Bullseye*.) The man's name was Leonard, and years later he'd be immortalised as Bolton's longest-serving paper boy in an episode of *That Peter Kay Thing*.

The real Leonard wasn't a paper boy and he didn't carry a giant cross around the town centre, but like his fictionalised namesake he was a religious man and his house had a small fairy light-covered cross in the front living-room window with a bright pink Robin Reliant parked outside. He would wear socks and sandals, even in winter, and a maroon sweater with Jesus Loves You emblazoned across it.

'I'm not sure if he was mentally unstable or anything but he was a nice chap,' says Marc Rowlands. 'All the local kids used to hang out at his house drinking cider and smoking cigarettes. I suppose he was the sort of person mums and dads would worry about being a bit dodgy, but he was totally harmless.'

For most of the kids, who were too young for pubs and too old for playgrounds, Leonard's house was somewhere to go. But for Marcus and Peter it was different. 'He wasn't very well and they looked after him a bit,' says Marc. 'They'd ask if he needed any shopping doing and stuff.'

Leonard was a regular visitor to the garage and, whenever he was there, Peter would tape their conversations together – a habit that had started several years previously when he recorded the family chit-chat over a Christmas dinner. 'Peter used to create situations to push Leonard's comedy buttons,' says Michael Atherton. 'I remember once he did a word association game, during which Peter called out ' "Brian Cant", to which the slightly deaf Leonard replied, "Hitler's book".' Asked what fascinated him about Leonard, Peter Kay replies: 'He had a lust for life. Everyone used to think, "Keep your kids away from him", but he were nothing like that. It taught me not to judge a book by its cover.'

The last time Peter and Marcus saw Leonard he was rescuing a cat from a tree. The next day he died. He had always told them how he had loads and loads of friends, but when they attended his funeral a few days later, they were the only ones there.

For the next seven years Peter would be in and out of 14 other part-time jobs ('I was never a full-time person') but his evening shift at the garage would remain a constant. He emptied bins for the local council; worked behind the bars at the Blur Boar pub and Yates's Wine Lodge; priced up tins of beans with mini-meatballs ('4p a can') and worked the tills at budget supermarkets Aldi and Netto. When he revealed the latter to a journalist from the *Scotsman* in 1998 she asked: 'An Italian comedy duo?' 'Nah, they're supermarkets for poor people. Really sad places.'

His employment history followed a familiar pattern. He'd stay for four months then either leave at the end of his probation period or get sacked for slacking or having a laugh when he should have been working. At Take Two Video, the small video rental store behind the Spar store in Deane, he once changed the labels on a kids' movie and swapped it with a porn film.

His other employment misdemeanours are the work of comedic licence. At Netto he says he was fired after he'd called his supervisor 'a dyslexic bitch' but he only told people this to set up the punchline that she'd misspelt her report to the Human Resources department; he lost his job at the Bolton Octagon box office for telling a customer he couldn't come in wearing white jeans: 'I was only joking'. Of course it didn't help that the customer was Phil Middlemiss, who played Des Barnes in *Coronation Street*; and at Yates's he got the boot for attempting to put a head on a pint of lager.

The reality, of course, was a bit more ordinary. He was disciplined for mucking about. 'I just spent more time eaves-dropping or listening to people than I did really getting involved in the job,' Kay admits. 'Whereas other people would be having an eye on the supervisor's job or seeing how much they could do in a day, how much stock they could shift. I wasn't lazy, I was just interested in having a laugh and not taking it too seriously.'

At work Peter felt like an outsider, as if he wasn't really supposed to be there, but his detachment from wanting to join the rat race was countered by a fascination with the people who did and the mad characters who populated every workplace.

Peter's first job was in the autumn of 1989, when he spent four months working at F. H. Lee's, the toilet paper processing plant known locally as Franny's because it was owned by the former Manchester City footballer. Franny's, which was only a few hundred yards from Peter's home, employed about 120 people, among them plenty of eccentrics. Maddest of all was a stocky chap in his thirties who favoured enormous turn-ups and was nicknamed Disco (due to his part-time mobile DJ business) who once put the forks of his stacker truck through a 22-gallon tub of glue and who at a works 21st birthday party tried to incorporate fire eating into his act but ended up causing thousands of pounds' worth of damage when he sneezed mid-performance. Once, attempting to put a spin on the old pub trick of tossing peanuts in the air and catching them in his mouth, Disco tried to do the same with money and ended up swallowing 10p. There was also an elderly gentleman called Cliff who owned three wigs – one for work, one for Saturday mornings when his job was to clean the machines, and one for Friday night out. His extravagance on hairpieces didn't extend to footwear – despite the pain, he used to wear a pair of shoes that were two sizes too small because he got them cheap in a sale. Looming over everybody, though, was the boss, Francis Lee's older brother Arthur. 'He just loved shouting at people,' says Mick Hall, who worked at F. H. Lee's for 24 years before switching to social work. 'It was all about production. If he caught you sitting down you were in big trouble. He caught me sitting on a couple of logs of paper in the back of the machine once and for that I was transferred to Manchester for three-and-a-half years. Mind you, I was sat there with my feet up having a brew and reading the paper.' Arthur Lee's favourite term of endearment was 'cocker', a word the workers would invariably hear as he guided a new recruit around the factory on their first day: 'Follow me, cocker, follow me.'

Peter's job was a simple one. He was one of the four workers who would wrap, glue and pack the toilet rolls as they emerged from the log-cutting machine. The three middle-aged women he worked with, who would talk openly all shift about their relationships and families, made up for the mundane nature of the job. For Peter it was comedy gold dust, and he'd rush home at the end of his shift and jot down all the conversations. Sometimes the things he heard were so good he'd sneak off and scribble them down on bits of cardboard – taking notes was a hobby. Women, he believed, were much funnier than men, who'd just talk about cars, football, shagging and getting pissed. 'Women are uninhibited; they tell you how they feel. The women at Franny's would talk about what they dreamt about one minute then operations the next.'

How Peter ended his time at Franny Lee's is unknown. Sometimes he says he was sacked, other times that he left when they shifted to continental shifts at Christmas – and he refused to wear a sombrero! 'He wouldn't have been sacked,' argues Mick Hall. 'If you worked at Franny's you were there for two weeks or the rest of your life. It was that sort of place.' Sombreros it must have been then. And toilet roll packing's loss was to be British comedy's gain.

After Franny's Peter moved on to Booker Cash and Carry on the Stonehill industrial estate in Farnworth, where he'd work in the afternoons a couple of times a week and then all day at the weekends. He was a favourite with the women in the cash office, Julie and Pat, and the ladies on the tills – Moira, Gina, Miriam and Sonia Hurst, who was known to him as the boyfriend of her sister-in-law Catherine Hurst. Their relationship lasted for three years after school but fizzled out when Catherine started dating someone else.

'I'd known Peter since he was about 14; he used to baby-sit my son, he were always a character,' says Sonia. 'He even DJ-ed at my wedding – well, if you call it DJ-ing – and he did my son's second birthday party, which was a joint do with Catherine's dad's 50th. Peter always told me he was going to be on television,' she says. 'When he made it nobody at the Cash and Carry would have been surprised; he had us in stitches. Whenever anything different came in, like bonsai trees, he'd always have some comment that would crack everybody up.'

Everybody, that is, apart from the Farnworth branch

manager, Brian Shacklady – a man in his late fifties preoc-
cupied with his thinning hair and, far more importantly,
shelf-stacking techniques. Peter would impersonate
customers, particularly the women, but his most successful
impersonation was of Mr Shacklady, who would endlessly
repeat phrases such as 'if you've got time to lean you've got
time to clean' at his more idle staff. 'He was one of those
people who would terrify you,' says Sonia Hurst. 'But he was
a character and all. If you were shelf stacking he'd come up
to you and say, "That's a good seller that, put it at eye level.
Eye level is buy level." ' Despite most of the staff being
scared of their boss, Peter didn't take him seriously,
repeating Mr Shacklady's 'eye level is buy level' mantra
whenever he was out of earshot.

Peter Kay's time at the Cash and Carry marks the only
time in his life when he experimented with his hair. He tried
to grow it long, but instead of growing downwards it grew up,
resulting in a horrific Curtis Stigers-style mullet. According
to Sonia, 'It gave him right grief; we said, "Get it cut, for
God's sake." ' She also remembers how Peter would get into
trouble occasionally. 'He'd make light of everything,' she
says. 'It would never be enough to get a written warning.
Sometimes I don't think he realised the boundaries.'

This was more than evident when Booker's became the
venue of some real drama one Thursday evening, when
armed burglars raided the store. Customers scurried under
pallets and staff lay flat on the floor with their hands behind
their backs. Meanwhile, Kay was pricing up some tuna in
brine with another employee, Kevin Broughton, on the other
side of the store when he suspected something was up from
the panicky voices blurting out of the Tannoy. 'We ran round
the corner and they were in front of us with these sawn-off
shotguns,' he told Michael Parkinson in October 2002. 'It's
delayed shock isn't it; two days later I was sobbing in the

middle of *Tomorrow's World*. They said, "You two, get down."
And I swear I went, "What, like dance? Get down, eh Kev?" I
thought we were all going to be on *Crimewatch* and this'd be
my big break into telly, but it was an inside job. Then I got
bollocked for putting in the time book – 4 p.m. to raid.'

After completing his Performing Arts BTEC at Bolton
College, Peter was supposed to return there to study for his
A-levels and, because he came from a low-income household, was given a small grant. However, despite starting
them he didn't see the course through, opting instead to
spend his grant cash on a coat and do a college open video
course for one afternoon a week. But when his friends
announced their plans to continue student life and go to
distant universities he began to wonder whether he was
wasting his life away. Not wanting to be left out or one to let
his situation get him down, Peter enlisted the help of his
friend's forgery skills and a borrowed *Roget's Thesaurus* and
spent an evening at the Esso garage applying for courses.
He'd asked his tutors for references but they'd declined, so
he decided to do his own. On the UCCA and PCAS forms he
wrote that he had A-levels in psychology and English literature and five GCSEs. The reality, of course, was that he
had just one GCSE, in art. He applied for a BA course in
Drama, Theatre Studies and English Literature at
Liverpool John Moores University and to his amazement
got an interview and then, after they failed to check his
credentials, a place on the course.

Liverpool University posed several problems for the 20-
year-old. First, new digs on the campus 38 miles from home
represented the first time, apart from holidays, he had spent
away from his parents. Hours after his mum and dad had
dropped him off at the university, he was back in Bolton
watching telly with his tea on his lap. His first lecture wasn't

for a week and he didn't see the point of hanging around when he could have been at home. The second problem, as befitted a student who had no qualifications and 'apart from *Charlie and the Chocolate Factory* and *Ferris Bueller's Day Off* on my holidays' hadn't read any books, was that he was hopelessly out of his depth. After floundering for the bulk of the first year, he made the decision to downgrade to a more hands-on Performing Arts Higher National Diploma (HND) course at the Adelphi College in Salford. The location meant it was nearer to home, but another feature of the HND course had caught his imagination: a 10-week module in stand-up comedy. After attending an interview and completing the task of writing a review and writing and performing a short sketch, he got the news that he'd been accepted for the term beginning September 1994.

It had taken a long time for Peter to admit that he could maybe make a living out of being funny – taking the carrot of the stand-up comedy module at Salford was the accept-ance of it. As he would explain many years later: 'I always wanted to be a comedian. You're naturally funny and there's a lot of egotism around that people go, "Oh so you think you're funny do you?" If you're a good mechanic or a good carpenter people accept it, but if you go, "I'm funny", people go, "Oh ay, Mr Big Head." I'm just good at making people laugh, I always have been, and I didn't want to be a 70-year-old sat in front of the telly going, "I could have done that. I'm funnier than that." '

In between leaving Liverpool and starting at Salford Peter would have to endure what he soon labelled 'the worst job of my life'. The summer of 1994 was memorable for two reasons. First, Wet Wet Wet were at number one for all 15 weeks of it with 'Love is All Around' from the soundtrack of *Four Weddings and a Funeral*. Second, it was one of the warmest ever. Not that Peter Kay noticed; he spent the entire length of it inside a windowless shrine to gambling, geriatric style – or, as he put it, 'I spent the summer with the cast of *Cocoon*'. He worked every day at the Top Rank Bingo Hall opposite the market in Bolton from 8 a.m. to 11 p.m. behind the bar, as a runner checking winning calls and as general dogsbody. Each day he'd leave his house in Croston Street and walk down the hill into Bolton listening to the James album *Laid* on his personal stereo – it was his habit to borrow cassettes from the library and he liked this one so much he renewed it over and over again and it'd become a ritual that he'd turn the corner to start each day with it. He didn't enjoy the work, but the mundane obsession of the bingo players, who'd dab their number grids with giant marker pens, and the blinkered worldview of some of the staff tickled him. Among them was head caller and manager Tom Henderson, a bingo veteran in his late forties who would make his arrival onstage to Tina Turner's 'Simply the Best'. He loved the tricks some of the old people had, like asking for a glass of water then topping it up with orange squash from bottles they'd later sneak out of their handbags under the tables. Peter was fascinated: 'I soon began to learn that bingo was a world unto itself, that it was much more than just a game. People would change when they came into the place, they would become aggressive and territorial, and we're not talking young ones, we're talking about the fragile and elderly members of our society. They were addicts. They were hooked. I remember one woman collapsed, she keeled over in the morning, they sent for an ambulance, they took her away to the infirmary, they gave her some tests, she woke up, discharged herself and was back in the bingo hall later that night in time for the National. That's how bad it was.'

The National was a game in which customers would buy special cards for a nightly bingo session where the whole of the Top Rank chain would link up to play one big game for a pooled prize fund. This was the hall's big money spinner and the bosses demanded complete silence from the staff, as the numbers would be broadcast by telephone over the Tannoy from the host hall in Wigan or Liverpool, a system many of the bingo players struggled to hear. One night Peter Kay found himself in trouble when he made too much noise stacking glasses, and towards the end of the all-important game he was called into the management's office for a telling-off about his slack attitude. The caller Tom Henderson asked him what his plans were in life. Aghast when Peter told him he was about to do a degree in Performing Arts, the caller allegedly replied, 'Have you no ambition? Don't you want to be a caller?' To which Kay replied, 'F*** off, it's bingo.' The pair continued talking while Kay kept one eye on the clock, mindful that arguing the toss was more fun than actually doing any work. 'Why do we keep on having to go through this?' asked Henderson. 'Because I've not clocked off yet,' replied his cheeky employee. 'That's another £1.25 you owe me.' When he emerged from the meeting he told his fellow staff waiting in the staffroom: 'I've just had an internal examination.'

That summer he also began a job with a brilliant perk – free cinema tickets – when he took a Sunday job as usher at the ABC cinema on Bradshawgate in the heart of Bolton town centre. In a previous incarnation it had been known as the Lido Casino and had been opened in a grand ceremony by *Coronation Street* actress Pat Phoenix, but in 1994 its glamour days had long gone and it was affectionately known locally as the flea pit, with good reason. Its down-at-heel nattiness didn't worry Peter Kay; he liked the fact that it was decaying and clinging on in the era of out-of-town multiplexes. At one point there had been 21 cinemas in Bolton; now there was only one. He loved everything about it, from telling his mates the endings of movies as they walked in to the local urchins who attempted to run away with a life-sized Gene Hackman standee just for a giggle, to eavesdropping on the ladies who worked behind the confectionery stand and cleaned the toilets.

'One day,' he recalls, 'Pamela was working in box office while Marie was changing roller towel in loo, so she said to a customer, "I'll tear your ticket here because Marie's upstairs changing her towel." And this chap looked disgusted and said, "That's more information than I needed, thank you." You couldn't write that, could you?'

After a summer spent almost entirely in the dark – dispensing free cups of water to the bingo ladies and watching *Forrest Gump* eight times in succession – Peter Kay emerged into the bright late summer sunshine of the Adelphi College building at Salford University. Contrary to popular opinion, the sun does occasionally shine in Greater Manchester.

'I'm not sure if it was the stand-up comedy element that caught his eye,' says Salford lecturer Lloyd Peters, who ran the module Peter Kay chose to incorporate into his two-year diploma. 'I know he was looking to get away from Liverpool. At the time it was getting a lot of publicity; I did quite a lot of interviews on the radio about it, although Radio Five got it into their heads that this was all we did, that students would spend their whole university life telling jokes to each other.'

As if! In fact a much greater part of the course was theatrical production, stagecraft and acting, and prior to his stint on Lloyd Peters's much-hyped module he appeared in several plays, including Euripides' Greek tragedy. *Electra*, where he played Tutelus, and, most notably, Nikolai Gogol's parody of Russian corruption *The Government Inspector*, in which he was given the lead role as the Mayor in three performances at the Adelphi Studio Theatre.

'He was wonderful,' says Lloyd Peters, who directed the Gogol piece. 'In fact Maureen Lipman, who was a visiting professor at the time, came to see a rehearsal and she picked him out. He did a lot of improvising around the script, which threw some of the less quick-witted members. I encouraged him to extemporise, which he grasped immediately.'

When it came to teaching stand-up comedy, Lloyd Peters was convinced that Peter Kay had done it before and was dumbfounded to discover that his only performance had been a best man's speech the previous summer.

'You didn't have to teach Peter much at all,' he says. 'I suppose another reason the module was quite attractive to him was that he knew he wouldn't have to study to get a good mark. A lot of the things I told the group – like keeping a notebook of jokes and ideas – he'd been doing for years. It involved a lot of homework, writing material, but Peter didn't need to, he'd have it all written already. In fact he was always helping other people with their acts.'

Peter was popular, but in a different way to how he'd been at school or at the Esso garage. Rather than fêted as the class clown or as someone who could blag you endless supplies of KP crisps, he was sought out because, according to Lloyd Peters, 'people recognised his talent'. Secretly though, the Peter Kay comedy recorder was still switched to 'on' and the middle-class students, especially those with artistic pretensions, fascinated him as much as the ladies on the assembly line at the toilet roll factory had done a few years previously. He noticed the limp way they smoked, their hand gestures and their liberal name-dropping. Like everyone Peter had spent time with, they too would find themselves incorporated into his comedy in the future.

Not that he spent much of his spare time at university indulging in the standard student pastimes of binge drinking, watching *Betty Blue* and experimenting with joint-rolling techniques. Peter Kay was far too busy working, and in his second year at Salford took on yet another part-time job: working Thursday nights as a steward at the newly opened Manchester Nynex Arena (later to be known as the Manchester Evening News or MEN Arena). On his first night there – Torvill and Dean's 'Face the Music' tour – the supervisor neglected to have a badge made up with his name on, so he had to wear one that read Mohammed instead. The day of his 22nd birthday in 1995 lived long in his memory, because prior to the show that evening the stewarding team staged a mock evacuation of the arena. And the music playing over the speaker system as they shooshed fake concertgoers from a venue they were supposed to imagine was ablaze? 'Burning Down the House' by Talking Heads. You couldn't make it up! All this was brilliant potential material for his first stabs at stand-up comedy; rather than make stuff up, he'd recount tales from the cinema and the arena, including the seminar he had to go on where two long-in-the-teeth security guards warned them of the dangers of flash photography and that 'men should search men and women should search women', to which one shady, bearded wannabe steward eagerly enquired: 'Can we frisk kids?'

On the stand-up course they would study other comedians, master microphone technique and write 'improvised' responses to heckles – Peter's was 'A penny for your thoughts. Sell! Sell!' Peter was interested in comedy history and fascinated by Peters's story about the time Danny Kaye had performed at the London Palladium and during the interval had remained onstage drinking a cup of tea and chatting to the audience instead of disappearing into his dressing room.

Sessions would begin with Lloyd Peters asking them to read a newspaper and pick something out to make a joke about. 'Reading a newspaper was quite a novelty for some of them! I'd tell them, if you can make a joke about the

European Community you can make a joke about anything.'
He would also get them to open up about their lives at home,
about being bullied at school or about their parents. Some
found it hard, but for Peter it would all come tumbling out.
He was on home ground; he'd been talking about this stuff
for years.

'For such a young lad he had amazing observational skills,'
says Lloyd. 'I think it was his working-class roots that gave
him this maturity that I didn't see in the other students. The
things the rest would dismiss – such as the price of pop they
were selling at Netto, where he'd worked – he saw as comedy
fodder.'

Kay was no less enthusiastic, later telling people that for
the first time in his life he'd found something that he loved,
that he was good at. Kay's tutor was also struck by his
knowledge of TV and by the fact that he knew about TV
shows someone his age really had no right to. When he
discovered Peters had a collection of 1960s TV theme tunes
he nagged him to lend them to him then incorporated them
into his act.

Part of the course was developing what Peters calls 'a
comedy persona' – either a character or a heightened version
of themselves. But despite this he believes that with Kay
there was less of a dividing line between the onstage Peter
and the offstage. Indeed, later on in his life Peter would
insist that he was more himself on a stage than off it. 'All
this theory and practice we did,' says Lloyd. 'With Peter? He
just went up there and did it.'

The culmination of the course was a show in the function
room at the Pint Pot pub in Salford, a regular comedy venue
near the university, where each of Lloyd Peters's students
would perform a ten-minute set and be marked accordingly.
Peter Kay came away with a Distinction, but it wasn't the top
mark. 'He actually got a D minus minus, which he was really

disappointed about. There was a guy who got a D, which is a higher mark, who was hopeless for eight weeks but then suddenly found his voice and was absolutely hilarious.'

Thinking he was the star of the pack, Lloyd Peters gave Peter Kay headline billing, but he ended up penalising him because rather than perform the statutory 10-minute set, his routine lasted closer to 45. He was also marked down for a slow start, Peters having taught him the importance of making an early impact.

After leaving with his diploma Peter toyed with taking up the offer of joining the final two years of the BA course, but with Lloyd Peters's advice to get an agent ringing in his ears he declined the chance and in the words of his mentor 'got out there and did it'. In his teacher's mind at least there was no doubt that Peter Kay was going to become a star. 'It comes along so rarely that when it does come along you know it.'

Kay himself was less confident, and he fell back into his old routine of working at the garage and the cinema. But he did keep his hand in at the theatre, and Sue Reddish of the Bolton Octagon Youth Theatre, aware of the achievements of a former member, asked Peter if he would adapt and direct the group's summer production based on *The Year My Voice Broke*, an Australian film about a boy watching his first love bloom into womanhood and fall for the charms of an older, insensitive brute instead of him. Because the play was for a cast of just four characters and there were about 25 kids in the youth group, Peter created a party scene so that everyone could have a part. It was like the film with a bit of *Home and Away* tagged on. Because they were all kids a box-office employee was roped in to play the lead character's father.

The play, staged on 23 and 24 August 1996, was successful with both performances selling out. When Peter Kay, Reddish and the box-office team went out to celebrate a day later – at Peter's suggestion to the karaoke evening at the nearby

Wagon and Horses pub – they found themselves there at the same time as an engagement party. Eyeing up the party's buffet bar, Peter managed to negotiate a deal where he would do some stand-up in return for some of the buffet. Impressed with his cheek, the young bride and groom to be agreed and, in return for a sausage roll, a couple of vol-au-vents and a pile of Skips, Peter Kay performed his first gig in Bolton.

Chapter Three
Move Forward Eight Spaces

'To get a job where the only thing you have to do in your career is to make people laugh – well, it's the best job in the world.'
Ronnie Barker

'I'd like to apologise to viewers in the north. It must be awful for them.'
Continuity announcer, Victoria Wood: As Seen on TV

Peter Kay's stand-up routine in exchange for a plate full of buffet wouldn't be his last professional engagement. After graduating from Salford University and spurred on by his friends at the garage, he telephoned a middle-aged gentleman known as Agraman for advice. Ten years earlier Agraman, whose real name is John Marshall, had ambitions to become a comedian himself and, not knowing quite how to go about it, started his own club in the function room of the Southern Hotel in the Manchester suburb of Chorlton-cum-Hardy. A lover of puns, Agraman (an anagram of anagram) named it the Buzz Club to complement the *double entendre* possibilities of the suburb's name. Numerous big names had been through the Buzz – Caroline Aherne, Steve Coogan, Eddie Izzard, Harry Hill, Jack Dee and Alan Davies had all played there early in their careers – with Agraman as the resident compère. Over the years Marshall had become something of a local comedy legend, a man who had been there at the start of the stand-up comedy explosion. He was also regarded as one of the nicest men in the business. Comedians, every one of them – even in the north, where we imagine comics to be take-me-as-you-find-me, unruffled sorts – are a self-doubting, suspicious bunch, but the niceness of Agraman was something they could all agree on. Even if his puns did make you groan – 'Shakespeare walks into a pub. The barman says, "You're bard."'

On 5 August 1996 the Buzz was due to host a heat of the coveted City Life Comedy Awards. Marshall suggested, on the phone to the young Boltonian, that he enter – all he needed to do was send in a cassette of his performance and if he thought it was up to scratch he'd be in. Such was the boom in local comedy that the alternative, waiting for an open-mic slot at the Buzz – amateur comics' usual route into the club – would take about seven months. Without any proper gigs to his name, Peter Kay decided instead to put his dictaphone down in a pub and record his conversation with his friends. Despite the unusual approach, Marshall was impressed enough to call him up.

'It was funny but there was a little bit of choice language and stuff like that,' he says. 'I rang him up and said, "If you do this sort of laddish stuff in the competition it's not going to go down very well".'

On the night of the show Peter Kay got the number 22 bus from Bolton to Chorlton and arrived at the venue jangling with nerves. 'It were a bit intimidating because I'd never done it before. And all the other comics who were there were like, "How long have you been doing this, son?" And I told them it was my first time and they said, "I don't think you should be here." But I had a go, like.'

'His name was randomly selected to go first,' remembers John Marshall. 'He went onstage and he was just about the Peter Kay we know today, an absolute natural; he won it by a mile. I've never come across that before or since: someone so fully formed at such an early stage in his or her career. I'd had people like Eddie Izzard and there were signs of what they would become, but no one was as natural or near the finished article as Peter Kay. And I'd never seen anyone come on first and win; that in itself was remarkable.'

In its six-year existence the City Life Comedy Awards had grown in stature in the north west, not because of its prize of £200 and a £20 HMV voucher, but as a stepping stone to greater things. The 1991 winner, Dave Spikey, who would compère the final at the Levenshulme Palace nightclub, had appeared and narrowly lost out in Jonathan Ross's prime-time *Big Big Talent Show* and landed a slot as the presenter of a daytime quiz show *Chain Letters*. But the real star to emerge from the contest was the 1990 winner, Caroline Aherne, who had appeared then as the foul-mouthed nun Sister Mary Immaculate ('How many Protestants does it take to put in a light bulb? None. They live in eternal darkness'). It was, though, another of Aherne's creations that had turned her into the most acclaimed comedienne of her generation. Disguised as the lovely elderly lady Mrs Merton, Aherne hosted her own chat show. Behind her blue-rinse wig, Aherne was as sharp as a tack and managed to touch the raw nerves of her guests with far greater success than TV veterans such as Michael Parkinson and Terry Wogan with their cosy knee touching. It signalled the end of the chat show, but it was hysterically funny, and for added effect her entire studio audience would be full of pensioners who were too old to know who half of the celebrities were and spoke their minds without brakes. Famously, Mrs Merton once asked wittering magician Paul Daniels's wife Debbie McGee: 'What was it that first attracted you to millionaire Paul Daniels?' And to feminist Germaine Greer she said, 'You were a right old slapper in the seventies, weren't you?' While Bernard Manning was simply asked, 'Are you a racist?' To which he replied: 'Yes.' Afterwards he claimed it was a trick answer!

Mrs Merton was Peter Kay's favourite programme in 1996, so he was somewhat alarmed to find her creator sat amid the faded glory of the Levenshulme Palace. Like everyone else in the swelteringly hot venue on Wednesday, 25 September 1996, Caroline Aherne was there to witness what was considered a foregone conclusion: the crowning of a spectacularly overweight comic from St Helens called Michael Pennington whose *alter ego* Johnny Vegas was causing huge excitement in Lancashire with a comedy routine that somehow incorporated a potter's wheel, masturbation and an audience rendition of the Frank Sinatra standard 'New York, New York'. Further stiff competition came in the form of Jenny Ross, who was fresh from sharing the first prize BBC New Comedy Award at the Edinburgh Festival with Marcus Brigstocke.

'Johnny Vegas was just brilliant,' says John Marshall. 'The audience loved him, but it was a long evening.'

'There were ten acts and Peter went on last when the audience was very, very tired and very pissed,' says Dave Spikey. 'He always reminds me that just before I introduced him I said, "It's all right, ladies and gentlemen, there's only one left." Then he came on and blew them away. Stormed it.'

'I was one of the judges in the final that year,' says Agraman *alter ego* John Marshall, who joined last year's winner Chris Addison and Palace owner Lawrence Hennigan on the panel. 'It was very difficult to decide between Peter and Johnny. They were both fantastic.'

'I got involved in the judging because they didn't know what to do,' says Dave Spikey. 'I couldn't understand what the problem was – there could only be one winner.'

'There were a lot of shocked people there,' says Marshall. 'Those that hadn't seen Peter in the heat thought it was a foregone conclusion that Johnny would walk it.'

The next day the *Bolton Evening News* reported their local lad's triumph under the headline 'Peter Becomes a Master of Mirth'. 'With members of the audience flagging as the night approached its conclusion,' they reported, 'Peter woke them up with his incredible fast and furious routine mixing quick-fire gags, hilarious observations and ad-libbing, feeding off a raw nervous energy. There was enough material in his 20 minute set for at least three performances, such was the speed of his delivery.'

Gauging the mood of the audience, Peter Kay had completely changed his style for the City Life final. In his three or four previous attempts at performing in front of a live audience he'd attempted a dry, slow style. That was now gone for ever.

'I just wanted to wake the audience up, so I speeded things up,' he told the local paper. 'I'm still a bit bewildered by it all. I couldn't believe it when I was announced as the winner, because I was up against some people who had been on the circuit for six or seven years.'

Immediately Peter Kay's world was turned on its head, and adding to his jobs at the garage and the cinema he now had a run of comedy gigs to keep him busy. Within a week of winning the City Life Award he appeared at the Manchester Boardwalk, the Frog and Bucket in Manchester and the Rubber Chicken Comedy Club at King George's Hall in Blackburn. Winning meant that he went from a nobody to a known act at an unprecedented rate. 'It was like move forward eight spaces,' he says.

'I was absolutely blown away by him,' says John Marshall, who since giving up the Buzz Club now books acts for dozens of venues in the north of England. 'Aware of how good he was, I gave him some one-man shows at a place called the Dancehouse Theatre in Manchester. People said, "Peter Kay? Never heard of him." And it was a real struggle to begin with. I barely got it half full, but by the time he'd been on twice we put him on again and sold out. I was happy in the knowledge that I had a real winner on my hands with Peter. He was brilliant value; you knew he'd bring in the customers and his sets would just carry on. He'd do the work of two comics and you'd only pay the one fee.'

Kay, though, couldn't believe the money he was earning: 'I remember being at my nana's after the City Life Award and being told on the phone, "I can give you £30", and me thinking, 'Bloody hell! £30 for 20 minutes. I used to work all week at the cinema for £42.50." '

It was at the cinema that Peter met Susan Gargan, a Boots cashier from the neighbourhood of Deane. A pretty red-haired girl a couple of years his junior, she'd been to Mount St Joseph's too, although the bulk of her time was spent at the new building. They got chatting and she decided to go and watch him play a gig at the Jabez Clegg in Manchester. The next night the pair went on a date to Blackburn Ice Arena, but they ended up spending the bulk of the evening in the Casualty Department of Blackburn Royal Infirmary after Peter slipped on the ice and broke his arm. 'Thankfully it didn't put her off,' he says. More pressing was the fact that he had gigs to play the rest of the week.

'Everyone thought it was a prop, waiting for me to pull out a bunch of flowers. They spent the first five minutes just pointing and knocking each other and going, "Watch this!" and then I started to really struggle because they realised that it was broken and I wasn't going to do anything – nothing spectacular was going to come out of it.'

Peter Kay was lucky to be coming through when comedy in the north west was going through a renaissance. Spurred by the success of *The Fast Show*'s John Thomson, Steve Coogan and Caroline Aherne, Manchester felt it was at the centre of rock 'n' roll comedy. Yet, despite the power base shifting slightly from London towards the north of England, the venues in Manchester and Lancashire in 1996 were far from ritzy – performing in a smoke-filled L-shaped pub, the stage would invariably be a crate, there'd be no microphone and your choice of lighting would be on or off.

Speaking with the benefit of hindsight, Peter Kay claims that he misses 'the smoke, and the adrenalin and the sick and the closeness' and reveals that he told jokes faster because he was scared of being bottled off: 'You've got to keep moving, you've got to be a fast target, chucking it out at such a rate, otherwise they will kill you. I've seen comedians forcibly ejected out of clubs, I've seen people have their hair set on fire, I've seen people projectile vomited on, and it's all good stories, and it's all a strange way to earn your living, and it's very much like a zoo and a circus. I was very frightened of Manchester then,' he says. 'I was very frightened of the Manchester comedy scene; everything that it stood for put the fear of God into me.'

Times were changing, though, and while every pub in the city was attempting to catch the wave with its own comedy night, established clubs like the Frog and Bucket, once 'so rough you'd think bouncers chucked drunks in rather than out', were moving to bigger locations, while the Boardwalk and the Hacienda, previously known as rock venues, were hosting regular stand-up nights too. It was an anarchic period, but out of all the acts appearing regularly in the city Peter Kay was the one who was beginning to bring his own crowd with him. Even so, he still suffered from hecklers.

'Heckling's a very male thing,' says one of Britain's finest stand-ups, Adam Bloom. 'If you're playing to an audience of nearly all men, it's horrible because you're almost obliged to pick on someone and to beat them as an alpha male thing. It's really ugly.'

Peter's method was to invite hecklers onstage, all the time

hoping that they wouldn't accept his offer. 'But I've found it's best to humiliate them,' he says. 'Talk to them like a teacher: "Now, this is all just a bit of fun, why are you so upset?" They usually slink away.'

Not that he didn't appreciate a good heckle himself. Once when he was working as a compère of a talent contest in Liverpool featuring a very poor impressionist, in the middle of his Terry Wogan impression, Kay mockingly shouted out: 'Do Wogan.'

David Perkins, manager of the Frog and Bucket, remembering Peter Kay's early gigs, says: 'He was always so focused. You could tell he was special. When he was compère I got so many complaints – not from the audience but from the other comics. They said they couldn't follow him onstage – he was just too funny. One night he came onstage dressed as a lion – a really fed-up lion with a fag dangling in his hand ...'

And it wasn't just any lion suit, either; it was the Cowardly Lion suit from his school *The Wizard of Oz* play. In the years to follow this suit would become something of a talisman for Peter, and it would make cameo appearances in nearly everything he'd do – from Bolton to Amarillo, it would never be far away. Some people carry a letter or a photograph to remind them of who they really are. Peter Kay dresses as a lion. In fact he only has to look at it and it'll make him laugh; transport him back to cocking his leg up a tree.

'The whole place fell about,' says Perkins. 'It's still one of the funniest things I've ever seen. As I run a comedy club, that's saying something.'

Perkins, whose Frog and Bucket is now one of the most successful independent comedy venues in Britain, says he knew immediately that Peter Kay was different from all the other comedians who had passed through his doors, that he was 'special' and 'focused' in a way he'd never seen before. 'I knew he'd be massive,' he says. 'Even back then, he said he wanted to be on telly – half seven on a Saturday night.'

According to one comedy agent of the period, who would prefer to remain anonymous, other comics at the time hated those evenings at the Frog and Bucket when the rising star was compère and she became accustomed to hearing her client's complaints. 'A compère has to take all the flak and heckles and ease the path for everyone else on the bill; they're not meant to be the star or hog the limelight,' she told me. 'The skill is to make everyone else look brilliant, but Peter Kay would want to be the star. He would do things like say, "Well, we've got another act coming on now, sorry about that, but I'll be back in a minute." '

Among his favourite playful tricks to sabotage his fellow comedians' routines was to take the microphone stand, lower it and tighten it to the point that when they came on they'd have to spend the first minutes, like a grandmother trying to open a jar of marmalade, trying to adjust it. 'First impressions are all important,' she says. 'And if you're wrestling with a microphone when you should be telling jokes it's likely that the audience will start thinking, "This is rubbish; we want Peter back." The first time I was told about it I thought that's a bit wanky; the second and third time I was like, "Oh my God, that's the most brilliant trick in the world." I'm laughing, but the comedians? Let's just say it pissed on their chips.'

According to seasoned compère John Marshall, the microphone trick is unpleasant and fairly standard in the profession and certainly not done exclusively by Peter Kay, but he says, 'He didn't make a great compère, he liked the limelight too much. You never felt as if you ever got to know Peter at all, that was my impression. He wasn't somebody I warmed to but he wasn't somebody I objected to either; you're not quite sure who the real person is. I was never sure whether he liked me or not.'

Peter's professional backstage oneupmanship went unnoticed by his audience, of course, who warmed immediately to his natural style, his tales from the mundane world of part-time work, memories of kids' TV shows and his gimmick of playing back songs he'd heard on the radio on his dictaphone. He was engaging and charming, and while other comics seemed to be about confrontation, he just wanted audiences to have a good time. It was hardly a radical idea, but most people don't want conflict and aggression at a comedy gig – they just want to have a laugh.

In his early sets Peter did a great spot about misheard lyrics, playing David Bowie's 'Let's Dance' and asking the audience why Bowie was singing about 'Les Dennis', and do Sister Sledge really sing 'Just let me staple the vicar' rather than 'Just let me state for the record' during 'We are Family'. It wasn't the most original of ideas, but it didn't matter.

The bulk of the comedians on the north-west comedy circuit overlooked some of Peter Kay's trickery and put it down to youth and inexperience. Dave Spikey spread the word on Kay wherever he went, while Adam Bloom – a rising star of the era – told an interviewer, 'Peter Kay is the most natural performer I have ever seen.' There was also approval from the older northern comics still on the scene. After a gig in Rochdale, Kay was invited to the house of Irish jester and 1970s TV icon Jimmy Cricket, famed for his ' … and there's more' catchphrase, and was delighted to find his red *This is Your Life* book suspended inside a glass coffee table in the living room.

Meanwhile, Oldham cabaret act Billie Bedlam, who was taking his routine of playing TV themes on a gigantic tuba and cracking gags around the northern circuit, saw something he liked in the 23-year-old Boltonian: sartorial correctness. 'Most comedians at that time would be wearing a denim jacket and holding a beer bottle,' he says. 'Peter wore a velvet jacket. There was no effing and blinding. It was very much a throwback to people like Les Dawson; you felt he'd be around for a long time.'

But if stardom, sartorial correctness and Saturday nights on BBC1 seemed his birthright, Kay's first attempted step into TV in September 1996 was an utter disaster. Charged with booking comedy acts for ITV's Friday-night competitor to *TFI Friday*, the Anthony Wilson-fronted *Welcome to the Candid Café*, young researcher Dawn Panton toured Manchester's comedy venues looking for new talent. Johnny Vegas, Hovis Presley and Paul Edwards were all booked to appear in front of a panel at Granada's Manchester studios to decide who would appear as the resident stand-up on the show doing a five-minute routine every week. Peter Kay, who had been recommended to Panton by Lucy Porter, a budding comedienne and researcher on *The Mrs Merton Show*, joined the hopefuls.

'She told me he did this great routine on commercials and kids' TV, so I went to see him at the Jabez Clegg in Manchester,' remembers Panton. 'He was brilliant, but when he turned up at the audition he was dressed in a white shirt and a suit like it was a job interview. He looked really nervous. When he came out of the audition he was white as a sheet, sweating and shaking like a leaf. I asked the producers what they thought and they said, "He's rubbish." They said he kept fiddling with his hands all the way through. I got chastised for it and told to pull my socks up. But they didn't like Johnny Vegas either, they said he was crude.'

This shared failure was one of many times the paths of Peter Kay and Johnny Vegas would cross in the late 1990s. Invariably they would be mentioned together when anyone needed to make a point about the north being funnier than the south – a fallacy as sweeping as that claiming Northerners as friendlier. For a short period in 1997 the pair even planned doing a double act together with a view to taking it to the Edinburgh Festival. The sole performance of this momentous event was at a Midlands branch of the Round Table. Hours of Internet research result in one eyewitness report; it reads, 'They died on their arse.' Wisely, Vegas and Kay went their separate ways. For a while at least, however, they remained friends, and when they met in Nottingham in 1999 prior to a gig at the Old Vic, the *Independent* journalist Brian Viner described their hug as 'an impressive engagement of northern blubber'. In his book about the history of British comedy, though, author Ben Thompson claims that around this period Johnny was so enraged that Kay had been given a series by Channel 4 and he hadn't that he broke 'a room full of pots in an orgy of unhappiness'.

Rather than join forces (or stomachs) with Johnny Vegas, in early 1997 Peter Kay found a comic partner closer to home. The compère of the City Life Award show, Dave Spikey, had kept in touch since his victory and had employed him to write the links to a daytime quiz he had found himself presenting. In the emerging comedy world of Kay and Vegas, aged 46 and white-haired, Spikey was classed as a veteran. He'd certainly waited a long time for his break and even despite his TV presenting job had retained his job as chief medical scientist at the Bolton General Hospital – by day examining the 'genetic abnormalities of haemoglobin', by night telling corny jokes about coppers in kids' playgrounds: 'Two policemen sat by a seesaw. I said, "What happened to you?" "We've been tipped off." ' Spikey had been trying to make it as a comedian for years, but his handful of gigs in working men's clubs had been disasters and he'd had little luck sending scripts to the Two Ronnies', Russ Abbott and the Grumbleweeds. He'd even spent a summer opening for one-time Saturday-night institutions Cannon & Ball at the Blackpool Opera House. Sadly, he fell out with them in an argument about alternative comedy, which the born-again Christian double act deemed the devil's work. 'It's all eff, eff, eff. There's nothing funny about that,' were the words of the diminutive moustache-sporting legend that still is Bobby Ball. 'They say they're God's crusaders for comedy,' says Spikey. 'Then they'd go onstage and do homophobic gags – "He's a woolly woofter, he's a poofter." Double standards, or what?'

Thankfully, Spikey broke into the alternative scene when he met John 'Agraman' Marshall and played the Buzz – 'it was an epiphany'. Then, in 1991, at the insistence of the Chorlton promoter he entered the *City Life* Comedian of the Year competition and won, but until his compèring gig at the 1996 final and the offer from daytime TV that came off the back of his Jonathan Ross endorsement, things had been moving slowly.

Chain Letters was a daytime quiz show where the lyrics to the theme tune explained the simple concept of the show: 'Take a word … Change a letter … Do it again … And you've got a chain/Chain Letters!' Dave's job was to wear a shiny suit, flirt with the guests and encourage their chain-letter-making skills. With five shows filmed every day back to back in the Newcastle studios over a two-week period, Spikey needed as many jokes as possible to fill up his opening routine and between-round banter, so he decided to offer the job to Peter Kay. Tailoring his material to the daytime nature of the show, Peter penned family-friendly gags like: 'Bloke goes to a fancy dress party with his girlfriend on his back. His mate says: "What are you going as?" The bloke says: "A snail". His mate points at the girlfriend and says: "Who's that?" Bloke says: "That's Michelle." '

Sadly, no film exists of the most momentous moment in the series, one that is still remembered fondly by daytime quiz show lovers and fans of rude words alike: 'I remember a taxi driver from Manchester who was trying to beat the clock in the "Superchain" final,' says. 'He changed the "r" in "cart" to an "n" for "cant". Then said, "I'll change the "a" to a "u" to make … er … can I do that?" We stopped the recording and I just had this big C*** flashing behind me.'

After *Chain Letters* Spikey and Kay wrote a few rough scripts together (including a long-held idea of Dave's of a sitcom set in a local newspaper) and sketched out a few ideas for shows and took them up to Tyne-Tees Television in Newcastle. Nothing came of that meeting but on the journey back to Bolton they hit on an idea for a Lancashire version of *Coltrane in a Cadillac* – a 1993 series that had followed the extra-large actor Robbie Coltrane on a road trip across America in a car as enormously proportioned as he was.

For a short period in 1997 Granada TV, the north-west ITV region, which operated out of studios in Manchester, took Peter Kay under their wing with a view to developing some of his ideas. They enrolled him on a directors' course, where he was pleased to find another Salford graduate and Aspects Theatre player Sian Foulkes, with whom he'd appeared in *The Government Inspector* and *Electra*. Together the pair worked on a script, and then when he heard of a new Granada series called *Mad for It* – a series exposing people's mad obsessions like topiary or Wild West shoot-out re-enactments – he fleshed out his and Dave's road trip idea. Titled *Mad for the A6*, the final show saw the pair travel in a weather-worn VW dormobile from Buxton to the Lake District on their favourite stretch of tarmac – *en route* this somehow entailed attempting to dress a Jersey cow in a raincoat.

Despite playing to a small late-night audience, *Mad for the A6* convinced Granada to cast Peter Kay in *New Voices*, a series of one-off dramas intended to showcase emerging new talent. 'Two Minutes' was written by Johanne McAndrew, who would later create the private detective series *Nice Guy Eddie* for Ricky Tomlinson, and directed by

Jonathan Campbell, who would go on to direct *Shameless*, *Spooks* and the movie *Alien Autopsy* as well as the first series of *Phoenix Nights*. In 'Two Minutes' Peter Kay starred as a shortsighted getaway driver so incompetent he'd bought a decaying Vauxhall Viva rather than steal a decent car. His fellow armed burglars (played by Matthew Dunster and Pearce Quigley) were equally hopeless, choosing a bleak pub in the middle of an industrial wasteland to rob and then being outwitted by the ageing clientele. It was a neat, tightly scripted film that didn't allow much room for improvisation, but Kay impressed with a brilliant array of astonished stares as his accomplices revealed their flawed plan. 'Maybe we should rob a garage instead,' says Dunster when all three are still in the car. 'Or a chippy, I'm bloody starving,' pipes our man from Bolton.

'I don't have to do this for a living, I just do it for the luxuries like bread and shoes.'

Les Dawson

In less than a year Peter Kay had gone from a comic known only to an exclusive group of Boltonians to Manchester's best-kept secret, headlining sell-out nights at the Frog and Bucket and the Buzz. He'd travelled down to London to appear at the famous Comedy Store, but suffered at the hands of a few drunken members of the audience – he emptied a pint glass over one customer ('there were only a bit left in it')and threatened another with a fork ('I was going to throw it at him'). Fortunately Comedy Store managing director Don Ward found it hysterical. Even so Kay returned lambasting the London scene as McComedy, with comics simply doing their 20 minutes and then buggering offstage when their time was up, disappearing to another club to do exactly the same 20 minutes. 'If you go over in London, they bollock you,' he says. 'I remember doing the Comedy Store and I was supposed to be 20 minutes, and they come up to me and say, "Twenty-two, you did 22. We said 20, you did 22'. Up here, in most places, they'll take the batteries out of the clock, or they'll kind of put you in a position where you can't see the clock or stop it, because the more they go over, the more they're rubbing their hands together, because they're getting more for the money, so if you do 40 minutes, there's your 80 quid and thanks – but in London it's the other way round, and it's funny.'

London comedy, then, was deemed fast food; the northern circuit was a full meal. In fact, often, this was literally true as many clubs in the north offered pastie and pea suppers with the price of admission or, as the Frog and Bucket did, an evening called 'Curry and Quips': a chicken tikka with added jokes. What could be better than that? For Peter the other advantage of local dates was that he could drive home after a gig and get home in time for *Prisoner Cell Block H*. If he harboured ambitions, making it big in London, let alone Hollywood, was not among them.

'A lot of comedians sleep on people's floors,' he tells William Cook in his book *The Comedy Store*. 'I don't like doing that. If I wanted a life like that I'd go and work in an all-night garage like I used to.' Subsequently Peter would turn down many offers of gigs at the Comedy Store. London's streets may be paved with gold, but given the choice he'd rather be at home with his mum cooking him a cauliflower grill.

For someone to eschew the bright lights and big money pull of the capital at such an early stage in their career was seen as both incredible and arrogant by some of his fellow comedians, but despite his whirlwind year he still had little belief that he would make it as a comedian or as an actor, and so kept his jobs at the cinema and Manchester Arena, which included all five nights of Take That's final tour – 'they were fantastic'. In his words: 'One minute I'm making thousands of people laugh, the next minute I'm picking up Toffos.'

Among the regular places he played in his first year was the Levenshulme Palace, where he'd won the City Life Award. The venue held a special pull for him and he'd often used unbilled nights there to road-test new ideas. Among them, one night he pulled a TV set on casters on to the stage with him and played a tape of old TV adverts he'd collated at home to the audience, commenting on each one. At this point he was making all his own bookings himself, keeping the dates in a pocket *Angling Times* diary given to him by his old boss at Chris's News. He had an acting agent, but when he phoned them in the summer of 1997 to ask if they had any work for him, they offered him a two-week job filing at their offices. Then when they did find him some work in a Chekhov play in a small theatre in Middlesex he found himself feigning a sore throat to get out of it. At that point, he says, he was 'terrified of straight theatre'. Instead, he found himself taking on stranger gigs. In Birmingham he performed at a policeman's party. When they heckled him by chanting, 'Who ate all the pies?' he responded by asking them, 'Shouldn't you lot be out arresting wrong Irishmen?' He also played a Christmas party for Blackburn taxi drivers – organised for June because they were too busy over the festive period. 'They had a Christmas tree and decorations and a DJ with a party hat on playing Slade. But there were only 14 of them there. Typical bloody taxi drivers, most of 'em never turned up.'

Joining the trend of stand-up comedy shows that summer was a new Channel 4 series called *Gas*. Hosted by comedian Lee Mack, the idea was to feature British comedy acts deemed to be off the wall and with an edge. Producer Sandie Kirk and assistant producer Lisa White organised auditions at comedy venues around the country. From London Lennie

Beige and Martin Bigpig got their breaks, while at the Manchester showcase at the Frog and Bucket Kirk and White selected the surrealist Noel Fielding, future star of *The Office*, Mackenzie Crook in his guise as end-of-the-pier entertainer Charlie Cheese, and Peter Kay.

Among such madcap company Peter Kay must have seemed decidedly straight, but for Lisa White he shone out immediately. 'I was blown away,' she says. 'For somebody so young, who had been doing comedy for only a few months, he was amazing.'

Just before *Gas* was screened in July, Lisa White decided to supplement her TV work by becoming an agent for the Off the Kerb agency. The first person she called was Peter Kay.

With an agent on his side the money started improving and so did the offers. That year he appeared on every stand-up show going, including BBC1's *The Stand-Up Show* and ITV's *Live at the Jongleurs* and *Last Laugh Show*; suddenly 'women in leggings' who never gave him the time of day before started acknowledging him – 'Ooh, we've seen you on telly.' Meanwhile, Lisa White had entered him into Channel 4's 'So You Think You're Funny?' competition and the BBC New Comedy Award at the Edinburgh Festival in August, both events that would, she hoped, bring in more work.

A week before leaving for Edinburgh, Peter Kay did his first TV interview for a late-night ITV show called *Funny Business*, telling the show's host Iain Coyle, 'I've never been to Edinburgh before, except when we went to the Isle of Rhum with the school and that was just to buy a Twix from John Menzies.'

'We were based in London but it was a Granada show, so part of the deal was that we had to do some of the shows from the north. I didn't know anything about Peter Kay when I arrived in Bolton,' says Iain Coyle today, from the set of *Big Brother*, where he works as a producer. 'Originally we wanted to interview Johnny Vegas, who was causing quite a splash at the time, but he had this over-protective agent so in the end he wasn't allowed to do it.'

Unable to agree on a venue for the interview and what with the weather being unusually fine, Peter Kay suggested they film it in the back lane behind the house he still shared with his mother. The first half of the interview takes place with Peter Kay wearing some disturbing Bermuda shorts and sitting on a deckchair. Neighbourhood kids clamber on walls behind him, attempting to get into the shots – 'Watch yourself with that bike, you'll have your eye out,' he turns round and yells at one point. Then to a lad, all of seven years old, in shorts flexing his muscles behind him, he tells Coyle 'he used to be in Jo Boxers, him'. This was Peter Kay caught to a tee, funny without even trying and remembering reference points that everyone else had forgotten about years ago – who else remembered Jo Boxers and the perky hit 'Boxer Beat'? Coyle was immediately impressed and stunned by Kay's encyclo-pedic knowledge of popular culture.

A few minutes into the interview the location switches to Peter Kay's bedroom, but what we didn't see outside was that the small wild kids who had populated the background earlier had been replaced by what Iain Coyle remembers as 'two heroin addicts' wandering up the street towards them. 'I saw them and I was terrified. But he dealt with them in the same way he dealt with the seven-year-old kids: he started talking to them and sort of taking the piss out of them without them realising. It was so funny how he dealt with them. They were like "What you doing?" and Peter said, "We're on telly, do you want to be on telly? Have you been on *Crimewatch* before?" One of the blokes was incomprehensible he was so off his head. Ordinarily I'd have run a mile because I was petrified, but he sorted it. He disarms people with his humour.' Safely ensconced in Kay's bedroom and surrounded by his collection of hand-labelled *Mork and Mindy*, *Only Fools and Horses*, *Porridge* and Genesis videotapes, Coyle was flabbergasted when he discovered that Kay still kept his Saturday and Sunday job at the ABC Cinema despite his run of TV appearances. But the comic told him it was good for material and started launching into his routine of the time.

'People phone up and say, "What's the queue for *Evita* like?" "A bunch of people waiting outside." These kids came in last weekend and looked at the kiosk and said, "Senior Citizens? What's that about?" I said, "It's like a Mexican version of *Cocoon*, now get out." People open the doors and lean in and go, "You haven't any idea what you're showing tonight, have you?" "No, no idea, mate, I haven't got a clue, I only work here." '

When conversation turned to famous Kays such as the Scottish comic Phil Kay ('like Billy Connolly with bulimia') and *'Allo 'Allo* star Gorden Kaye ('he used to work at the Bolton Octagon'), Peter remembered he had a *Tommy the Tuba* album by Danny Kaye and began rooting through his album collection to find it. 'There was just a wall of records and he had a stepladder to reach them all. He had an Evel Knievel album and really weird 1970s albums and all these reference points that were amazing.' Other records pulled out included German porn soundtracks by a chap called Otto Weiss (*Otto Weiss is Nice*), Tony Christie's *So Deep in the Night* and *The Collected Broadcasts of Idi Amin*.

Asked by Coyle whether his material was about Bolton, school, girls or sex, Kay replied: 'All of that – except the sex. I'm not a prude, but people say I'm very mainstream. I don't think I am but I like stuff that's funny and old. I don't think there's mainstream or alternative; if something's funny it's funny.'

He went on to say that not much made him laugh other than Ronnie Barker – an idol he would later exchange fan mail with (Barker sending Peter letters on HMP Slade notepaper). 'I'm more of a laughter giver than a laughter taker,' he remarked, stifling a giggle.

'I don't think he ever believed he was as good as he was,' says Ian Coyle now. 'But when I was interviewing him, he was almost like a Victoria Wood character. All the references and what he was saying, you could just tell he was going to do something great.'

As fate would have it Iain Coyle was about to play his own small part in Peter Kay's next brush with greatness when he managed to sell a programme idea about the Edinburgh Fringe Festival to ITV and accidentally became a comedy award judge.

Chapter Four
None of That Effing and Blinding

'I not only use all the brains that I have, but all that I can borrow.'

Woodrow T. Wilson

'Adrian!'
'Rocky!'
'Adrian!'
'Rocky!'
'Adrian.'
'Rocky.'

Talia Shire and Sylvester Stallone, Rocky

The Edinburgh International Festival began in 1947 and in the wake of the Second World War was given a perky remit to 'provide a platform for the flowering of the human spirit'. For most of the visitors this entailed watching a fireworks show and a spot of military bombastics, but seeking to take advantage of the crowds a group of eight uninvited theatre companies took over a disused pub on the Royal Mile and started staging daily productions – the Edinburgh Fringe Festival had begun. Decades later the Fringe – a mecca for experimental dance troupes and one-armed jugglers alike – had expanded to include a Comedy Festival which quickly became the stand-up comedian's equivalent of the World Cup. In the late 1980s, when alternative comedy was in bloom, comedians would centre their entire year on hour-long shows. By the 1990s TV producers were using the festival as a place to spot upcoming talent and do deals. It is also one of the few occasions all year when a rising star can find himself reviewed in a national newspaper.

As each year has passed the Comedy Festival has become less adventurous and less fun. Comedy is big business, but once you realise this it's harder to enjoy it. Countless careers have been launched off the back of successful Edinburgh runs: Stephen Fry, Frank Skinner, Eddie Izzard, Steve Coogan and Lee Evans all gained TV contracts after being nominated for the coveted Perrier Award. As well as these big names, hundreds of lesser-known acts pour into the Scottish capital like so much seaweed washed up on the shore, desperately hoping that some passing comedy bigwig or at least a couple of tourists from Canada will notice them. In 1988, as a way of encouraging this fresh talent, the founder of the Gilded Balloon venue, Karen Koren, started the 'So You Think You're Funny?' competition aimed at amateur stand-ups who couldn't afford to hire a theatre for their own showcases. The initial prize in its first year was £250 from Koren's back pocket, but as the years progressed and Channel 4 climbed on board the prize fund swelled to £1,500 and the biggest carrot of all was that commissioning editors from the TV company as well as journalists and radio producers would be watching. Despite Channel 4's involvement it still had an edge that the Perrier Award didn't; if the big-name comics were the major-league movers then the entrants of 'So You Think You're Funny?' were the far cooler, eager comedy underdogs.

Iain Coyle, from ITV's late-night comedy programme *Funny Business*, was overjoyed to find himself in Edinburgh interviewing various comedians in the Pleasance Theatre Courtyard – the main congregation point for ligging and revelry – one night. After being approached by one of the

Gilded Balloon employees he found himself roped in to judge one of the four 'So You Think You're Funny?' heats. He was delighted.

'When I saw the name Peter Kay on the running order I thought there's no point watching any of the others,' he laughs. 'Paul Foot was on as well and he was really good, but then Peter came on and just blew the whole place away. Afterwards you have to go into this little room in the Gilded Balloon and discuss what you thought, and me and Fred McAuley just went, "What are we bothering even talking about this for?" The people from the Gilded Balloon were going, "Paul Foot was very good." And Fred, who was on the panel with me, said, "Look, are you mad? If he doesn't win this, there will be a riot." '

At the final a few days later comedian Adam Bloom, who'd been a 'So You Think You're Funny?' entrant three years previously and was beginning to make a name for himself on the various stand-up TV shows, went along to the Gilded Balloon to check out this 'fat Northern bloke' everyone was raving about. One of Bloom's favourite acts, Paul Foot, had made it to the final as a runner-up but the other comedian Bloom remembers from the night was a Liverpudlian called Anton who was like a 'cross between Alexei Sayle and Steven Wright with some of the funniest one-liners ever'. The host was Julian Clary who, as usual, was adorned in glittering purple camp finery with vast shoulder pads and protruding peacock feathers. Clary's put-downs were as subtle as his outfits and, on withering form, every time he mentioned the title of the show he would make his thoughts clear on the proceedings by emphasising the word 'think' in 'So You Think You're Funny?'. Sadly, it didn't go well for Anton, who was overcome with nerves. To make matters worse he left his carrier bag of props on the stage and had to shuffle back on to collect them while Clary was in the middle of his between-act banter. 'Anton came walking back on to collect his carrier bag just like a passer-by would in a street,' remembers Adam Bloom. 'There was no respect whatsoever for Julian Clary in all his glamour onstage; it was as if he'd left his carrier bag in a café and was just going back to pick it up. Hilarious.'

After such a pitiful opening the stage was set for Peter Kay, who was on second. He didn't disappoint. Instantly Adam Bloom realised that the majority of the audience were here to see the Boltonian. 'He walked on storming,' he says. 'It was incredible; before he'd even got to the microphone the crowd were roaring. He'd won the audience over before he'd even spoken; I'd never seen anything like it. The other thing I remember was that he was wearing bright white, brand-new trainers, and I thought, "You should have scuffed them up a bit, mate." '

Peter Kay's set included a routine where he pretended to be a dad miming to the keyboard part in Soft Cell's 'Tainted Love', which is ridiculously basic and simple to begin with before it goes off on a spectral synth journey. When he told the audience where he was from, he remarked, 'Bolton, the only place in Britain where people still point at the sky when they see an aeroplane.'

'The room was in stitches. We all knew he'd won it when he came off; everyone thought no one's going to top that,' says Adam Bloom. 'But the real moment I knew he was going to be a star was when he came on to collect his prize. The stage had all the contestants on it, the people from the Gilded Balloon, Channel 4 people, the stage was crammed, and he was among them all with his award and he said, "It's like *Rocky* this," and he went "Adriiaannn". We've all seen *Rocky*, the ending when he's in the ring covered in blood; we're all emotional and he can't find his wife and he doesn't care about all the press and all the boxing industry, he just wants his wife. And I just thought to myself there couldn't be a more appropriate line for that moment and I roared. It was cocky because at the moment of humility – he'd just won an award – rather than say "I can't believe this" he carried on being funny. You could say that's slightly obnoxious because there's a time to just take it and be humble, but it was brilliant. The audience adored him. They're loving him already, he's won, then he hits them in the stomach with the *Rocky* line. And I just thought, "Do you know what? You're just too, too good." '

As if witnessing the 'So You Think You're Funny?' victory wasn't enough confirmation, Adam Bloom became certain Peter Kay was going to become a megastar when, a few weeks later, he found himself on tour with him. Comedy promoters Avalon had arranged a short stint at northern universities for Bloom and called him to say, 'There's this new bloke we think is really great. We want him to support you, he's called Peter Kay.' Their first gig together was at John Moores University in Liverpool, where only three years previously Kay had limped through a year as a student before moving to Salford.

'He turned up to the gig; it was the first night of the five we did and he was in the dressing room and he was sat there in the chair,' says Bloom. An expert in the slight nuances of human behaviour, the southern comedian detected something out of the ordinary in his fast-rising support act. 'There's a difference in status; whether you acknowledge kudos and hierarchy or not, it clearly exists. New acts don't make jokes at the expense of established acts in dressing rooms because there's a subconscious feeling that they might get their gigs pulled or miss out on a TV show. There's a pecking order, dos and don'ts, just like there is in any industry. Although he didn't say anything out of line, the way he was sitting in this chair looked like *he* was the star. He was just a man sitting in a chair, he wasn't lording it, he wasn't strutting, he wasn't smoking a cigar, he wasn't wearing anything special, he just looked like he had the presence about him, that he was a man who was about to go onstage to thousands of people, not 128. And I remember thinking, "There's something different about this bloke"; it wasn't arrogance, although there must have been a bit to make me think, "F***, I'm your support act!"

'If you just imagine being ushered in to meet God by a load of angels,' laughs Bloom. 'When you got there there'd be something in his posture that would be different to a normal person, yes? Now, I'm not saying the guy's a god, I'm just saying that the guy acted like it was his show. I slightly resented it,' Bloom adds. 'I'd appreciate that if you put the God reference in, you also put the resentment bit in.'

Like a confessional, Kay used the Liverpool show to own up to his sin of lying to get into the university. The students in the hall found it hysterical. But then he could have read out the Funeral Directors section of the *Thomson Local Directory* and people would have been in creases.

After each gig Peter would drive home, back to his mother's house in Bolton, while Bloom stayed in a local hotel. Just before their final date together at St Martin's Teacher Training College in Lancaster, Peter had to visit the hospital, and turned up at the gig with his arm in a sling. As ever, he turned what had happened into a part of his routine that night, but it wasn't so much the joke that impressed Adam Bloom as how easily he won over the audience. 'The poster for the gig that went out over the campus had me on it and no mention of a support,' he says. 'So he was unadvertised, there was no MC to introduce him and the audience had no idea who he was. He walked onstage, grabbed the microphone and told a story about the tube that had been put into his arm when he'd had this operation. He didn't look up at the audience, which is an extraordinary sign of confidence, and he trusted that his charisma was enough to make them want to listen and he told a story about the nurse putting a tube in his arm and she slipped and went, "Oh shit." His point was you don't really want someone talking like that just before they're about to operate on you. But the thing that blew me away and made me realise that he was going to be a star was that he hadn't even established himself with a hello, he hadn't made some funny generic comment about the room or himself, he'd just walked on unannounced, unadvertised. It was the Adam Bloom show, he was just there to warm up the crowd, and he walked on and within one or two seconds the whole room was his friend. They cared about his arm and wanted to know the story. I'd never seen that before in my life.'

After the gig Bloom regrets not approaching Peter Kay and telling him 'I bet my life you are going to be a big star and please give me 1 per cent of your future revenue in return for my confidence in you.' But he didn't. Instead, he went back to his hotel and tried to figure out how Kay had managed to charm the audience so easily and how, after three years in the game, with nothing but good reviews, he was being overtaken by a kid from Bolton.

The truth was Peter Kay wasn't like any other comedian on the circuit. The normal rules did not apply. 'He acted like a star who they loved and they just went, "Yeah, he's a star who we love." For me that's a mind-blowing level of confidence and belief in your likeability. I remember racking my brain to try and understand how it was possible. He had no fear.'

Adam Bloom ended the short tour with Peter Kay with mixed feelings. He was awestruck by Kay's confidence with the audience and was confident he had witnessed somebody with huge potential, but equally he felt aggravated by some of the tricks Peter Kay had pulled to undermine him. Kay was booked to perform 25 minutes each night, but at Lancaster after 15 minutes he told the audience, 'I'm sorry, I've got to go now', and waited for them to respond with an 'ahhhh'. Before the gig Adam Bloom had told him he could do 35 minutes if he liked, but getting the audience's sympathy, getting them subliminally to demand more was part of the stagecraft he'd picked up from Salford.

For Bloom it got worse. 'He said "I've got to go now" and the crowd groaned so he said, "Unless Adam Bloom will let me do some more." He left me in an extremely unfair position. Now I'm the Elephant Man's evil owner whipping him in the cage. I've already become an oppressor before I've even gone onstage – what chance do I stand now? Peter Kay is a very, very clever manipulator of situations and there's no way on this earth that he didn't know what he was achieving. That's my only beef with him. But I don't actually think it was anything more than another driver throwing tacks on to the racetrack behind him. I just ran over some of his tacks.'

Despite possessing superhuman evil comedy powers, back home Peter Kay behaved as if nothing extraordinary was happening in his life. If anything, away from the comedy clubs, he became even more normal. Conscious of his weight, which had climbed in direct correlation with his success, he joined Slimmers' World and attended meetings with his mother, Deirdre, every Tuesday evening. Those who recognised him there suspected they were being filmed as some elaborate candid-camera joke for a future TV show, but he weighed in with everyone each week and stayed for the motivational chats by the club organiser. Now, no longer working in factories and warehouses, it also gave him a chance to check in on regular conversations and keep his comedy hearing alert to some unintended comedy pearl. The low-calorie chocolate bars were also pretty good.

With the money he earned in Edinburgh from 'So You Think You're Funny?' and the BBC New Comedy Award he bought a second-hand Ford Fiesta and went back to his job at the cinema. Even when his manager Lisa White landed him a regular slot on BBC2's *The Sunday Show* he would rush from the studios on Oxford Road in Manchester to rip tickets and show people to their seats at the ABC in the afternoon. 'People would give me a double take and say, "Weren't you on telly just now? What are you doing here?" But I just liked it. Plus I got to see all films for free.'

'I don't sell the ice-cream,' he would add. 'People throw things at you and it's a girl's job – the union would be on to me.'

The BBC's Head of Entertainment Features, John Whiston, had been keeping tabs on Peter Kay for the past year and had even caught him at an end-of-term revue by Salford graduates the previous summer. With Channel 4 chasing Kay too, Whiston was keen to give him work, and as well as *The Sunday Show* he was hoping to develop a sit-com idea of Kay's called *Seaside Stories* which was to be set and filmed on location in Blackpool, Southport and Morecambe, following the adventures of coach parties of pensioners.

Quizzed by the *Bolton Evening News* on the eve of his debut on *The Sunday Show*, the local lad who 'still lives with his mum' appeared to be taking it all in his stride and told the paper: 'It's a thrill unlike any other to be presenter of *The Sunday Show*, an excitement that few people on this earth get to experience. Who would have thought that those bright lights existed somewhere over the rainbow.' Sarky bugger.

The Sunday Show was into its third series when Peter

Kay joined presenters Paul Tonkinson and Donna McPhail as part of the regular cast of a show designed to help viewers recover from the night before. He was joined by Jenny Ross – whom he'd competed against in the City Life Award Final the previous summer – offering a comic slant on showbiz news; and by Bez, the dancer from the Happy Mondays and Black Grape, whose enthusiasm for class-A drugs had once led him to be described as 'a walking medicine cabinet'. Here though, Bez was trying something different ... DIY. Each week, after he'd hammered together a shed or dispensed technical advice, he'd end on his catch-phrase – 'Job's a good 'un.' Kay was there to take the place of Dennis Pennis, Paul Kaye's brash American interviewer who had hung around film openings and asked celebrities like Demi Moore 'Would you ever consider doing a movie where you kept your clothes on?'

Although initially the production team at BBC Manchester wanted Peter to do short two-minute stand-up slots, he came up with 'Peter Kay's World of Entertainment' instead, where he would play dodgy old vinyl records or reminisce about old children's TV shows with the help of grown adults dressed as schoolkids. In one episode Billy Bedlam appeared – playing the theme from 1980s afternoon programme *Jonny Briggs* on his tuba as Peter goofed in the background.

'He were a bit raw,' remembers Billy Bedlam – a man who, among his many accolades, can rightly claim to be the world's fastest trombone player. 'But he was great at ad-libbing. He had to read everything off an autocue and I remember he really struggled with that. At one point he got it all wrong and just went up to the camera and started dusting the screen.'

With Dennis Pennis, who had been handed his own BBC2 series off the back of *The Sunday Show*, gone, *The Sunday*

Show was deemed low-budget trash by the critics and roundly ignored. For those lucky enough to see it, Kay shone. It had a huge and immediate effect on his popularity. A couple of weeks after his *Sunday Show* debut he performed at the Frog and Bucket in Manchester and the tickets sold out in a day, the manager telling the *Guardian* on 21 October 1997, 'We had to turn down 500 bookings.' The *Guardian* was the first national newspaper to pick up on the phenomenon of Peter Kay and, travelling to Bolton, discovered a comedian slightly disbelieving of his newfound celebrity, joking that the people who did make it into the Frog and Bucket gig 'even waited until the interval to go to the toilet'.

'Kay's style of comedy demands your attention,' wrote the reporter Collette Walsh. 'A bit like Dave Allen on speed, he reels out stories and observations about life and people: his family, old schoolteachers and staff at the cinema where he works are the main targets.' Despite being wide of the mark with the Dave Allen comparison, the *Guardian* got it right when they noted that Peter's audience was a lot more mainstream and not strictly limited to twentysomethings, like most acts on the comedy circuit. Peter Kay told them: 'It's just a matter of taking out the swear words I suppose. You have to read the audience to know what you'll get away with. I really don't see the point in offensive comedy. With *The Sunday Show*, I've got to watch my language; it's daytime telly and although it's assumed that hungover students are watching, there are probably kids and parents too. Anyway, people don't want to hear heavy Ben Elton stuff these days. I'm not into comics who go on about politics and sex, or who slag off their audience.'

To help him remember not to swear he jokingly asked *The Sunday Show* if they could put a cardboard cut-out of his mother in the row. Maybe they should have: his first words on air were 'I am the bastard son of Alf Roberts'.

Mrs Kay attended many of Peter's biggest shows and whenever he found himself swearing he'd always put his hand over his mouth and apologise. Indeed, in the early days, Peter indicated that his mother played a far bigger influence in his act than those impressions of her dancing to Sister Sledge. 'She's pretty cool, my mother,' he told the *Manchester Evening News*; 'in fact she writes half of my material.'

'When we were kids Deirdre had a good sense of humour,' says Peter's old schoolfriend Michael Atherton. 'She seemed to act as a kind of yardstick for things that might cross the line for being too sick or facetious. Peter's "impression" of her in his act, by the way, is fairly accurate.'

Deirdre Kay acted as a filter, attempting to remove the bad language from his act, but most people simply did not even hear it. 'That was one of the nice things about Peter,' says Billy Bedlam. 'He made it with none of that effing and blinding.' 'What I'm doing is really old school,' admitted Peter Kay at the time. 'I think if I'd come along and done this five years ago it wouldn't have worked.'

In an early profile in the *Independent*, comedy writer Simon Fanshawe said that the clubs of Manchester were 'not the natural habitat for this oversized, six-year-old-looking man-child of a comic whose face is too young to talk about sex, that kind of crowd's standard fare, or to swear, their staple vocabulary'. He wasn't that innocent, but there was something decidedly old-fashioned and uncomplicated about him. In response to the publicity about this 'new Alan Bennett' who looked like a young Alf Roberts with a clean-cut non-sweary act (ignoring the occasional slip-up), Kay noticed his audiences getting older. At one point a whole coachload of pensioners appeared at a Blackpool gig. 'It's like we raided Age Concern,' he joked.

This pan-generational appeal was something that Lloyd

Peters, the stand-up comedy teacher at Salford University, had noted in his protégé early on. 'Peter's gift was that he had lived a bit, so he had a store of material you wouldn't see in a normal young comedian,' he says. 'He worked as an usher, with the bingo crowd, he's worked and lived with old people and therefore has a whole range of old connections and observations about old people and how they live and work. The secret of his success is he connects with the old, middle and young age groups unlike any other contemporary comic, and that's his great gift, so when he got up and told jokes about old people's homes and how old people can't work answering machines it was from his experience.'

Graham Linehan, the Irish writer of the sit-com *Father Ted*, agrees. 'When you see his live show he will do impressions of old women at a wedding, for instance, and it'll be spot on, and then he'll do an impression of the six-year-old kid at the wedding and that'll be spot on as well. He's not isolating his targets to one particular age group. There are some comedians and they are just aimed at 16- to 35-year-olds, so it's acid and satirical and very ironic or clever; Peter Kay's clever but he's not trying to be clever; it's really, really intelligent, brilliantly observed, very sweet and very funny.'

'Peter Kay's genius is recalling a more innocent past,' says writer and broadcaster Andrew Collins, whose book *Where Did It All Go Right?* is chiselled from the same mound of childhood happiness as Kay's. 'I don't know how calculated it is, but he appeals to the part of us that finds the modern world confusing and depressing. Weren't things easier in the old days? His persona belies his actual age. He comes across as a middle-aged man, and always has done, and that endears him to older audiences. I have no idea why anyone under 30 would find him funny. But I have sat at suburban dinner parties and listened as people in their forties who don't even watch that much telly swap Peter Kay quotes, just as undergraduates used to with Monty Python. He really tapped into an older market.'

As Collins points out, Peter Kay was 'predestined to appear in *Coronation Street*.' The warm, gentle humour of the programme and Kay's reputation as a working-class comic with old-fashioned values meant he was a perfect fit for the show with its cobbled streets, corner shop and neighbourhood pub, something most towns and cities in Britain had lost decades ago. But his first appearance on the soap opera was a blink-and-you-missed-it cameo broadcast on 17 November 1997, in which he played a shop fitter helping Fred Elliot expand his emporium with a new shop sign and a few new cabinets – Fred's rival Maude sneaking a raw kipper inside one of them. 'Do you like blue?' asks Peter Kay in the background as Maude goes about her evil work. Peter Kay was only on screen for four minutes, but found himself being recognised and stopped in the street because of it and, as ever, started weaving his Weatherfield experience into his comedy set. 'They all talk posh,' he told his stand-up audiences. 'But they're putting it on, they are. Gail Tilsley's on the phone [puts on posh voice] – "Yes, well it will have to be two o'clock," and I'm like, "Stop it and talk proper." '

> We hate it when our friends become successful
> And if they're Northern, that makes it even worse
> *Morrissey*, 'We Hate It When Our Friends Become Successful'

As much as the public adores Peter Kay, his fellow comedians, who will groan and grumble at the merest mention of his name, loathe him. The root of their beef is that he uses other people's jokes without giving them credit. But when it comes to going on record with these accusations they clam up.

'I've got major problems with Peter Kay,' says one Manchester comic.

What are they?

'Do you think I'm mad? I do want to work again, you know!'

'He stole a joke off me once,' says one, reciting a popular Kay pun before backtracking: 'Please don't print that, he's richer than me.'

'Other comedians live in fear of him coming to their gigs,' says one Blackpool-born stand-up. 'Because you know he's watching for what bits of your act he can subtly change and make his own.'

Other current comedians cite a long forgotten act called Woody Bop Muddy, whose performances consisted of him playing a cheesy single on an old record player then ripping it off the turntable and destroying it in a series of inventive and violent ways. Peter did a similar thing on *The Sunday Show* – not every week, just once, but it is highly unlikely that he was aware of the obscure Muddy. Besides, Peter's taste for cheesy vinyl was established when he was twelve. The accusations demonstrate how far back some people in the comedy business are prepared to go to prove their point.

One London agent told me that she didn't feel Peter Kay used remarkably similar material to some of her clients maliciously. He just had a different 'old school' mentality to everyone else. 'In the 1970s you'd hear Bruce Forsyth tell a joke on the Saturday, then hear Tommy Cooper tell it again on a different programme the next week. It never used to be an issue. Jokes were seen as fair game; they didn't belong to anybody. Now, though, there's an emphasis on writing your own material.

'Mention Peter's name on the comedy circuit I'm on and people spit blood,' says the wickedly funny Glaswegian comedienne Janey Godley.

'There is a sense of resentment towards him, certainly within the London comedy world,' says comedy writer Andrew Collins. 'Having said that, there are few professions as insecure or paranoid, so perhaps it's nothing to do with what he does, merely that he did it outside the traditional radar. Perhaps because he arrived fully formed.'

Today, animosity directed at Peter Kay is expressed cagily in dressing rooms or behind the disguise of a nickname on an Internet message board, but when Kay was starting out in 1996 and 1997 they almost put a halt to his career. At the 'So You Think You're Funny?' heat in Edinburgh, Iain Coyle remembers that several of the judges were adamant that he shouldn't win because they'd heard several of his jokes before. 'The thing is, jokes aren't what makes Peter Kay funny,' he says. 'I remember talking to Paul Zenon, who was very big at that time, and he said that he'd take it as a compliment.'

Perhaps one of the reasons other comedians dislike Peter Kay so much is not that he tells similar gags to them but because he tells them better? When he was on tour at the tail end of 1997, another comedian at a Manchester date told him about the rumours. Discussing it two years later, Kay told Chris Oliver Wilson of *The Times*: 'When I started doing stand-up, a lot of comedians accused me of stealing their material. It really upset me. I was naïve. I didn't know there were a thousand other comedians talking about Jerry Springer and *Teletubbies*. So I thought, "Sod you. I'm going to talk about my family." Then comedians can't come to me and say I've lifted it, because they are my own stories and real things that happened. But there's still a lot of jealousy. They accuse me of lifting material. Some people are bitter because they had a career plan and it just hasn't happened for them. They begrudge other people having success.'

Janey Godley agrees: 'I like him, but other comics they'll say they like him then say that they want to kill him behind his back. It's the same with Jimmy Carr. For what? For being successful?'

Then as now there is a feeling that Peter Kay had it easy – that all the doors magically sprang open for him and slammed shut for them. Adam Bloom can understand the feeling towards Kay in the industry because, he says, 'For most comics overnight success takes ten years. The only other person I can think of who was as successful as quickly as Peter Kay is Jack Dee.'

Google a few of the corny gags Peter Kay tells at the start of any of his live DVDs and you will discover that many of them are also credited to one-line expert Tim Vine, some to Tommy Cooper and a couple to high-voiced American eccentric Emo Phillips. But discovering the origins of jokes, unlike song lyrics, is impossible – nobody copyrights gags. Muddying the water further is the fact that in the era of email forwarding, two lists – one entitled 'The Genius of Peter Kay', the other 'Peter Kay's Universal Truths' – have been circulating for several years. Despite being very funny and containing the kind of thing you can imagine Peter saying – triangular sandwiches taste better than square ones; you never know where to look when you're eating a banana – he wasn't the original author of either list; somewhere along the back lanes of what Clive James used to mockingly call 'the information super highway' his name got attached. The truisms originate from two ex-students from York, Tom Sharp and Andy Milson, who published them in a book called *100% True* in 2001.

Perhaps Peter Kay's attitude towards the end of his 'Mum Wants a Bungalow' tour in 2003 was the right one: to let the audience tell the punchlines to his oldest gags, like a joke version of karaoke. Jokes in themselves are not what makes Peter Kay funny; he is a brilliant storyteller, actor and observer of human quirks. Terrible cliché it may be, but never has the phrase 'it's the way he tells them' been more accurate.

'It's his ability to be loved onstage that makes him a genius, not his ability to write jokes,' says Adam Bloom. 'Woody Allen said a comedian's a funny person doing material and not a person doing funny material, and I think that's hit the nail on the head with what Peter is. He can say anything and be funny. Who needs clever twisty turny jokes when you can just be funny without doing anything? What an amazing way of being.'

Writing on the <chortle.co.uk> message board recently, Toby Foster – who had starred in *Phoenix Nights* as a member of the the Phoenix Club's backing band, Les Alanos – defended his friend from a fresh wave of allegations: 'PK is great at what he does, and a lovely bloke. Stupid personal attacks like this just make you sound like a c***. People seem to imagine that Peter was just hewn from some rock and bunged onstage at the Albert Halls to sell out crowds, forgetting the years he put into stand-up ... I can honestly say that I never saw him do anything other than storm in every club gig he did. A chancer? He worked his bollocks off, and became successful, that's the fact.'

Just as at the Edinburgh Festival, where Peter had made the audience laugh long after his act was finished by quoting *Rocky*, often the thing that people laugh most at is the bit after the punchline has been delivered – 'You can have that. You can keep that one.' It is both a Kay family trait he'd caught off his father and an excellent tool for leading into the next joke or section of his routine. Technically it's brilliant, and in a business that feeds off laughter, where an ordinary comic would get one laugh Peter Kay manages to get two, or three.

Peter Kay doesn't claim his work is 100 per cent original – on the DVD commentary of *Phoenix Nights* he admits borrowing some gags that he'd seen in other sit-coms, although he couldn't remember their titles. In fact, the one time Peter Kay has fully owned up to using someone else's material it was with a joke that got him the sack: 'I was on Preston train station and this announcement came on. Ladies and gentlemen, the next train is an express to Carlisle. We advise passengers to move away from the yellow line at the edge of the platform as they may get sucked off … bit of blue for the dads there, bit of blue.'

He told this joke during his spell as warm-up man on *Parkinson*, where he worked in January 1998. According to the *Daily Mail* it was allegedly Mary Parkinson, Michael's wife, who objected to the 'blue' nature of the gag (ironic though it was). Either way, he admits that being sucked off at Preston station was the reason he got the boot eight weeks into the job.

The person who got Kay that job was his Mancunian friend Danny Dignan, who was also Parkinson's producer. Being a warm-up man is a difficult task. You need to welcome the audience and get them to comply with the house rules – no going to the lavatory during recording, no leaving before the end, no heckling – and you have to keep them happy between the endless breaks for adverts, make-up and reshoots. Then, in the middle of one of your jokes, the floor manager will shout, 'Going to taping. Quiet please.' Not easy. These were all qualities that jarred some-what with Peter, and typically he saw the challenge slightly differently. As well as the guests on the show he wanted the audience to go home each evening remembering him, too. Not everyone on Parkinson's team found Peter perfect warm-up material. Michael Parkinson thought he was fantastic.

Peter described the job to the *Bolton Evening News* on Friday, 23 January as 'scary' and told them it meant that finally he would be giving up his usher job at the ABC Cinema in Bolton – finally, 18 months after winning the City Life Award, he had accepted he was a full-time comic.

'I have to follow people like Billy Connolly – it's very difficult,' he said. 'During every interval between guests I come on and talk to the audience. They usually use a comedian who has been in the business for about 30 years. To choose someone like me is amazing. But they wanted something a bit different.'

A perk was that he got to take his parents to the shows. His mother and nan travelled down to London for the Billy Connolly appearance and, as a 50th-birthday treat, he took his father along to a show where Phil Collins and John Prescott were guests. Backstage, before recording, Peter told them it was his father's birthday and Michael Kay was treated to a surreal celebrity moment as the former Genesis man, the Deputy Prime Minister and his son sang 'Happy Birthday' to him. It was a peculiar show that was filmed on Thursday, 5 February 1998 – Prescott breaking free of the normal expectations of a politician by going into the orchestra and playing the drums. Peter Kay's memory of the night, though, was the way in which his father spoke to the Hull MP. 'I remember seeing him and saying, "Hello John", whereas my dad said, "Hello, Mr Prescott." It's funny how different generations behave.'

Whereas other people in Peter Kay's position might have been star-struck by Parkinson's guests he treated them like regular mortals: 'I'd just say something like: "The kettle's over there." Seeing all these famous people was a bit strange. It was a bit like being in Madame Tussaud's, yet everyone was real.'

The day after the Prescott show, Peter was booked to play at the Comedy Store in the West End and took his father along with him, the pair having their photograph taken next to the sign outside the famous venue with Peter billed as the headliner. Kay's second performance there was a bigger success than his first – despite struggling against a noisy bar, he took it all in his stride. 'What's going on back there?' he asked. 'Someone got a car boot sale on or something?'

When his invitation to clap along to the *Jim'll Fix It* theme tune at the end of his set was met with a muted response, he asked the audience, 'What do you need? A metronome?' In William Cook's *The Comedy Store*, Peter says, 'I had fears that I wouldn't translate outside the north west.' But he had no need to feel afraid. 'It's the rhythm, isn't it? Sometimes you can tell a joke and if it's said a certain way they'll laugh even though they don't know what they're bloody laughing at. When I first started, I tried losing my accent,' says Peter, revealing that at his first show south of Birmingham, in Bristol, he'd tried to 'take the Northern out of my voice. It didn't work. I was self-conscious about it, but it turned out that it was one of my strongest things.'

This was more than apparent later in the year when Peter was approached by an American woman on the Royal Mile in Edinburgh who told the comedian: 'I thought you were really funny. I've no idea what you were talking about, but you made me laugh.'

Back at the Comedy Store there was another difference Peter noticed between himself and his counterparts on the southern circuit. In London there are so many clubs that acts can polish the same 20-minute set over and over again and never perform to the same audience. Up north, because there are considerably fewer comedy venues, Peter felt he had to change the act every night. He'd always take his tape recorder to gigs with him and record his shows – not only to see what bits got the biggest laughs, but also to ensure he didn't do the same act when he returned a fortnight later. His method wasn't to write his act but to have themes which he'd expand upon. In the first two years of his stand-up act part of the reason his regular followers loved him so much was that, unlike with so many comics, you never saw the same show twice. Despite the loose nature of his sets there was a structure. As he says: 'I always try and go full circle on a story. Then it becomes more like a piece of theatre to me.'

'That's the trouble with stand-up comedy: people want to hear jokes.'

Peter Kay, Live at the Comedy Store

Losing the Parkinson job was a minor setback to be filed away alongside all the other temporary jobs he'd lost. In fact it led to another warm-up-man job, this time on a couple of episodes in the first series of *Rolf's Amazing World of Animals* on BBC1. It was, says Peter, 'the easiest job I've ever had. I was supposed to fill in between all the technical breaks but Rolf would always appear to entertain the audience and I'd be sat there getting paid £200 to watch Rolf Harris play his didgeridoo.'

Rolf and Parky notwithstanding, 1998 was the year when things really began to step up a gear for Peter Kay – not that they hadn't moved quickly enough already. On Saturday, 23 May Channel 4 was due to air the terrestrial première of Robert Redford's movie *Quiz Show*. Building a whole themed evening around the event, the film was sandwiched between Bob Monkhouse with a personal history of his years as a game show host and, at 11.30 p.m., *Let's Get Quizzical*, in which Peter studied bizarre moments in quiz show history. It was a great programme, with Peter's links done from a mocked-up living room featuring him in a stuffed armchair as he played clips, such as the man who answered 'Turkey' to every question in *Family Fortunes*. Peter also astutely noted that Steve Coogan's Alan Partridge character was surely based on Fred Dineage, host of *Gambit* – a corny TV version of blackjack but with the added appeal of Fred and his glamorous assistant Michelle Lambourne (job description: hold giant playing cards and smile) flirting. In the clip Peter played, Dineage was revealed as a man who made it obvious that he assumed all TV hostesses were thick when he remarked, 'Michelle is the thinking man's Muppet.' Kay, an expert on UK game shows, having spent the bulk of his childhood weekends watching *3-2-1* and *Bullseye* as well as writing the jokes for Dave Spikey's *Chain Letters*, made the point that in order to appear on TV ordinary people had to be willing to have the piss taken out of them. To demonstrate the point he showed a scene of Bill Grundy hosting *In My Opinion*, a game in which three middle-class panellists had to guess a working-class person's political opinions.

'What is comedy? Comedy is the art of making people laugh without making them puke.'

Steve Martin

Having just gone to the Edinburgh Fringe Festival for three days to compete in the competitions the previous year, Peter Kay found himself having to find a temporary apartment in the city when he returned in 1998, as Lisa White had arranged for a full three-week run at Pleasance over the Road – one of the many outbuildings of the Pleasance

Theatre, the hub of the Comedy Festival. It was the longest he had ever been apart from his mother and away from Bolton in his life. The digs he hired weren't up to much; despite paying out a fortune (many Edinburgh residents hire out their homes during the festival at extortionate rates) he was appalled to discover that his landlord had left piles of dirty laundry everywhere. 'I mean my house is not much more tidy,' he said. 'But when it is someone else's it's different, isn't it?'

Edinburgh 1998 was regarded as a vintage year for emerging talent by many observers, including Nica Burn, the producer of the Perrier Pick of the Fringe, who compared it with the year when Emma Thompson, Stephen Fry and Hugh Laurie shared the bill of the Cambridge Footlights show. Among the buzz shows were several with surreal leanings that some journalists saw as a signal of the end of stand-up comedy. Among them were two comedians called Julian Barrett and Noel Fielding, who had created an off-kilter parallel universe called the Mighty Boosh in which they performed as two disillusioned zookeepers attempting to unravel the mysteries of the space–time continuum. Invited to join the debate about standard comedy's demise, however, Barrett and Fielding declined. 'It's ridiculous the way we keep on being asked on radio shows to slag off stand-up,' Barrett told *The Sunday Times* in an article headlined 'The Surreally Useful'. 'Why would we want to do that? We're not anti-stand-up; it's what we do for a living most of the time. You can't have a wild man dressed in strange fur with Polos instead of eyes running on to the stage in a stand-up routine, whereas we can in the Mighty Boosh.'

If anything, Edinburgh 1998 proved that regular mainstream stand-up, rather than weird comedy psychedelia, remained the dominant force. The angle was debunked even further by anyone who got the chance to see Peter Kay that year. Reviewing his show in the *Independent* on 27 August, James Rampton wrote: 'The Edinburgh Comedy Festival this year has been full of pontificators predicting the death of straight stand-up. But in Peter Kay's case, it is very much alive and kicking; in fact, it's in the rudest of health.' Rampton noted that Peter Kay's subject material of taxi drivers, bad DJs, *Bullseye* and the embarrassing way your mum dances at wedding receptions was hardly breaking any new ground but 'Kay gets away with his hackneyed choice of material by the sheer verve with which he performs it'.

Hackneyed or not, the audience lapped it up, and despite the slightly negative reviews, he was very much the people's choice when he was announced among the five nominees for the much-coveted Perrier Award alongside Canadian Sean Cullen, pub landlord Al Murray and two Irishmen, Tommy Tiernan and Ed Byrne. 'I am really, really chuffed to be nom-inated,' Peter told the *Bolton Evening News*. 'I'm confident – confident that I won't win it, and I know they all say that, but I do really mean it.'

Peter's hunch was correct. Among the Perrier voting panel there was a perception that Peter Kay didn't need it. 'There was a feeling that the Perrier was already too small for him,' one of the panellists later revealed. Possibly an additional factor was the fact that he disappeared for a week of his run to a former lock keeper's cottage in Bow, East London, and the set of Channel 4's morning show *The Big Breakfast*. With regular presenters Johnny Vaughn and Denise Van Outen on holiday, Kay (who'd impressed as a sharp-witted guest a couple of months previously) was invited to be a host for a week alongside Melanie Sykes, the actress and model who had shot to stardom on the back of her adverts for Boddington's beer ('by 'eck it's gorgeous').

Kay was worried that they were a beauty-and-the-beast combination. 'Have you seen the state of me?' he asked. 'Most of the viewers will be a sight better-looking than me.' But the pair quickly settled into their place as the north's answer to Johnny and Denise, Peter even developing a bit of a catchphrase – 'yes indeed, ladies and gentlemen'. It was a chaotic week, full of blunders – Peter stepped on Sykes's toe and left her gasping and he struggled with his autocue – but it all added to the anarchic fun of the show. One morning, hosting a game show within the programme on which three women appeared, he very obviously let one of them win – but then she was his girlfriend Susan! When the wind blew open the living-room curtains when he was mid-link he rushed to close them and in disgust at the weather shouted 'August!' at the camera as if he was a dinner lady worried about the weather at break time. At Channel 4 and among TV critics the verdict on Peter's *Big Breakfast* week was positive. On the Tuesday after the first show, Kathleen Morgan in the *Daily Record* wrote, 'While Vaughn is off, he should sharpen up his repertoire. He has some tough competition back home.'

It's tempting to assume that Peter's career took off on the back of Edinburgh 1998 (Channel 4's comedy commissioning editor, Katie Taylor, was among the judges on the Perrier panel) and his successful five days on *Big Breakfast*, but the wheels were already in motion long before. Sandie Kirk, who had produced the *Gas* TV series where Peter met his manager Lisa White, had been commissioned earlier in the year to develop a new strand for the channel called *The Comedy Lab* to encourage new names. The idea was that these new comedians and writers would put together half-hour shows – screened in the post-pub 11.30 p.m. slot – and hopefully one or two series would come out of them. The first person she approached was Peter Kay.

Chapter Five
It Smells Like a Rotten Alsatian

'Still to come, the man with the enduring twinkle. And that's
David Essex. Plus, the five-year-old boy who knows the name
of every motorway junction from Land's End to John o'Groats.
The amazing walking, talking map-boy.'

Judy Finegan, Richard and Judy

'There used to be a real me, but I had it surgically removed.'

Peter Sellers

Peter Kay's contribution to Channel 4's *The Comedy Lab*,
'The Services', was written mainly while he was in
Edinburgh in 1998 and while he was presenting *The Big
Breakfast* for a week in London. Earlier in the year, when the
offer had first been made, he'd surprised producer Sandie
Kirk, as well as Jack Dee's production company Open Mic
who were behind the series, by telling them he didn't want
to do a stand-up special ('mainly because I'd use up most of
my act', he told them). Instead, he saw it as a chance to do
some acting – and not the highbrow stuff his acting agent in
Manchester was still phoning him up about: 'Now I could do
comedy acting.' Kirk – who knew him only as a stand-up act
– was surprised, but gave him his head. After all, the idea of
The Comedy Lab was to give emerging talent the oppor-
tunity to express themselves, and the other episodes in the
series were no less adventurous – Dom Joly's *Trigger Happy*
pilot, which followed a week after 'The Services', with its

actors in giant squirrel costumes fighting in a shopping precinct springs to mind.

Peter began by developing further a rough script he had started with Sian Foulkes on the Granada TV directors' course and came up with the idea of spoofing the docu-soap genre that was overrunning the terrestrial TV schedules like a plague of ordinariness at the end of the 1990s – everyone from clampers to bin men were being filmed for the nation's fix of funny realism.

'I always used to love Victoria Wood when she did documentary spoofs on *As Seen on TV*, like "A Fairly Ordinary Man", "Winnie's Lucky Day" and "Swim the Channel". I thought that's what I'd really like to do,' he says. 'At the time there were programmes like *The Cruise* and *Lakesiders* and *Hotel* and I thought I really wanted to do something like that so I came up with the idea of a service station because I thought it was a really classless place – upper class, working class, they've all got to stop at the services. It seemed like the perfect place with so many people passing through from bin men to rock stars, from school trips to pensioners on mystery tours, it had it all – not to mention the staff.'

Originally Channel 4 wanted to film the show close to London. The budget for each episode of *The Comedy Lab* was around £40,000 and this had to pay for everything: cast, the crew (who were all based in the capital), catering, transport as well as the standard rate for first-time scripts (approximately £4,000 according to former Channel 4 employees). But first Heston services on the M4 wouldn't give Channel 4 permission, then every other service station followed suit. 'Because of all these documentary programmes dishing the dirt they all said no,' says Peter Kay.

At first Peter and Sian were faced with the unwelcome prospect of having to rewrite the script and set it in a supermarket instead. But then Channel 4 came back and told them that there were two independent service stations in the British Isles – one in Swansea and the other in Bolton, four miles from Peter's home – and they'd agreed to let them film there. Kay was chuffed; not only would he be filming locally, where his characters were based, but also First Services Bolton West was perfect because nobody ever stopped there, it was run-down and quiet. In other words 'a bit of a shithole'.

His *Comedy Lab* show was given the title 'The Services'. It came together with suggestions from Dave Spikey (who came up with the outline for manageress Pearl and the storyline about the missing French tourists – 'blooming French, they don't know a word of English') and Neil Anthony (who would later change his surname to Fitzmaurice), a Liverpudlian comedian Peter had become friendly with after they'd competed in the same BBC New Comedy final at Edinburgh in 1997. Neil had told him about a screenplay he was working on about a Liverpudlian gangster and told him, if it ever got made, there'd be a part for him in it. Although both Dave and Neil were uncredited when the show was aired, Peter made sure to mention them in interviews surrounding the screening. Ideas for what the characters should wear were fleshed out on the way to live dates in early summer – invariably with Paddy McGuinness who'd drive with Peter to some of his further-flung shows.

'I remember working it out with an A4 pad sat on a bed in a cheap £10-a-night B&B in Bristol,' says Peter. 'We were watching *My Cousin Vinny* with the sound turned down and I was sketching out a mullet hairdo.'

Three weeks before filming was set to begin the bulk of the script was yet to be written. In fact, Peter penned most of it during the holiday to Las Vegas he took with Susan after the Edinburgh Festival. Instead of gambling away his life savings or going to watch Siegfried and Roy getting mauled by white tigers, Peter spent the majority of the seven-day break writing in his hotel room, then wandering the Vegas strip attempting to find somewhere he could fax his final drafts to Sandie Kirk in London. 'It cost me £50 and I never got it back on expenses!'

Mind you, Peter and Susan did take some time out and lots of it wound up entering the stand-up shows he'd perform through 1998 and 1999. 'If you think I'm fat, you want to go to America; it's like *It's a Knockout* out there,' he tells audiences, miming some ten-chinned beast wobbling around a shopping mall.

In Las Vegas Peter also had his first taste of alcohol for years. He and Susan had gone along to a *Stars in Their Eyes*-style tribute show and, not wanting to waste the free drink voucher that came with the ticket, Peter ordered a Baileys because he likes Baileys-flavoured Häagen-Dazs. The result? Susan having to pull Peter away from the dancefloor as he danced like his dad to a Four Tops tribute band.

Most of the parts in the 25 minutes of 'The Services' were to be played by Peter Kay himself – partly because, as a fan of the Peter Sellers movies *Dr Strangelove* and *The Party*, he saw this as a comedy tradition, but also because he didn't trust another actor to pull off exactly what he wanted – and certainly not without being paid. Apart from Peter Kay and Sian Foulkes (who would progress to roles in *The League of Gentlemen* and *Emmerdale*), the only other actor in the show was Paddy McGuinness. McGuinness, Peter's schoolfriend who would give Foulkes the nickname 'Does she?' on account of how her name sounds with a Bolton accent, had two lines. 'Are we getting time and a half for this lot being here?' he asks, gesturing towards the unseen camera crew during a staff meeting. 'Standard rate, Equity, surely.'

'One word, Terry: Job Club,' replies the service station manageress.

The real staff of Bolton West Services and the customers became unpaid extras. Not that Paddy was really an actor either. Just as Peter had done, he was stumbling through a succession of low-skilled jobs, and after a spell as a building-site labourer was working as a fitness instructor and lifeguard at Horwich Leisure Centre. When he heard how much Peter was earning from his stand-up act he thought, 'I'll have some of that' and began hatching plans for his own comedy career.

'The Services' was put together extremely quickly, filmed over three days in October then screened on Channel 4 as the first show in the *Comedy Lab* series less than three weeks later, on Wednesday, 11 November at 11.30 p.m. There was just one review in the national press, by Brian Viner in the *Mail on Sunday*, but it was brimming with enthusiasm. 'The Services' was screened in the same week as Victoria Wood's long-overdue debut sit-com, *Dinnerladies*. Viner noted that *Dinnerladies* was all but welcomed to BBC1 by a team of buglers in gold smocks, which makes it a little unjust that "The Services" barely snuck on to Channel 4 before midnight, for *Dinnerladies* was nowhere near as funny.'

Brian Viner had been tipped off about Peter Kay during an interview with Caroline Aherne and Craig Cash, who were promoting their sit-com *The Royle Family*. In his review of 'The Services' he was quick to point out their shared 'acute ears for the absurd banalities, not to mention the banal absurdities, of everyday conversation' and also mentioned Steve Coogan, writing that Kay was 'blessed with a comparable genius. However, there is more warmth in Kay's characterisations than in Coogan's, and more humanity.'

In true docu-soap style 'The Services' centred on a typical day in an everyday workplace and featured a voice-over, by Peter, midway between bored and patronising, that was typical of the shows of that era. The spoof was completed by a generic saxophone instrumental even Kenny G would have found repellent. The characters Peter appeared as would all reappear later in his TV career, with the exception of Pearl Harmon, the bolshie service station manageress who believes the appearance of the TV cameras will be the start of her life as a celebrity.

In one of the early scenes we spy Pearl on the phone to her friend Carol, through the half-shut door of her life-sappingly dull office, boasting about being on TV. 'Look at the Mo, she only passed her driving test, she had a record in the Top 40 and they did her bloody life, did you see that?'

'I loved that line,' says Peter. 'People always say stuff like, "Did you see that Claire Sweeney on *This Is Your Life*? She hasn't had a life. She's only 12." '

As well as Pearl, Kay played Mathew Kelly – a customer care assistant in the final year of a drama degree who would rather be onstage than cleaning toilets: 'It smells like a rotten Alsatian. Why can't they flush, the filthy bastards'; Alan McLarty – a disgraced ex-employee of the RAC ('She was fifteen and a half, what's six months?') who has set up his own motor recovery service called the ARC and holds strong views on corporal punishment, believing that they should 'hang joy riders on the National Lottery. And when the body drops the foot sets the balls rolling'; Utah – a coach driver whose real name is Craig: 'Utah's my wild west name,' he explains; and Paul LeRoy – the mullet-haired 1980s-obsessed DJ staging a roadshow at the service station to drum up interest in his radio station Chorley FM. 'We've got a foot spa, health spa and a £20 voucher for your local Spar, so near so,' says LeRoy to an empty car park. 'Three fantastic prizes and all available today from Chorley FM, your favourite waste of time.' Cue – 'You're My Favourite Waste of Time' by Paul Owen.

Of the five, he admits that Mathew Kelly is basically Peter

Kay playing Peter Kay, albeit slightly camper and with an Irish accent – his thespian pretensions picked up by studying the mannerisms of the drama students at Salford University. In an out-take Kelly tells the cameras he's from the small Irish town of Coalisland – the birthplace of Peter Kay's mother, Deirdre. All five characters have classic scenes: Utah shakes the interviewer's hand and asks him to 'watch my trigger finger'; Paul LeRoy's impassioned paean to the 1980s – 'Every year something different happened' – as he played 'I Think We're Alone Now' by Tiffany to an audience of exactly zero; and best of all angry self-employed Scot Alan McLarty suffering a mental breakdown and last seen wandering down the hard shoulder of the M61, with his trousers around his ankles, singing 'We Will Rock You' by Queen. 'The police had truckers ringing up saying there's a madman loose on the motorway,' laughs Peter. 'But we had permission.'

After filming Peter revealed that LeRoy was based on a local radio DJ a friend had seen doing a roadshow at the far end of a Tesco car park once, while the inspiration for Utah was a coach driver he'd personally experienced while on a family holiday to Barmouth in Wales in 1991. This man spat a bottle of orange squash over his windscreen when he realised it was undiluted cordial and attempted to impress the teenage Peter Kay by referring to his coach as 'a big girl'.

'The Services' began two recurring motifs that would run throughout Peter's TV career. One was Chorley FM – Paul LeRoy's radio station with its unintentionally (by the fictional radio station) cheeky slogans 'Coming in your ears' and 'Where the listener comes first'. The other, rather bizarrely, was Bob Carolgees, who with his puppet Spit the Dog used to terrorise guests on the riotous Saturday-morning kids show *Tiswas* by gobbing on them. Such discourteous behaviour then was inspired by punk rock, but today, in an era where children are practically doused in tinned tomatoes the second they enter a TV studio, Carolgees's phlegm-based capers seem a little tame. In 'The Services' 'TV's own Bob Carolgees', as Pearl calls him, is an unseen presence but he still sends the staff into a tailspin when the manageress gets wind of his imminent arrival – the cynical Mathew Kelly even rolling out a red carpet and removing all the adult magazines from the shop.

'I don't know why we were obsessed with him,' says Peter. 'When we met him he asked about it, but I couldn't really explain it.'

The biggest surprise for Peter's friends watching 'The Services' and for those who had witnessed him performing in smoky northern clubs was seeing him convincingly pull off the role of Pearl. It was even more bizarre for Peter, because the make-up and Dorothy Perkins blouse turned him into the spitting image of his mother's sister, Auntie Bernie.

In the DVD commentary of 'The Services' Paddy McGuinness says that he finds it weird seeing his mate dressed as a woman, but Kay enjoyed the experience. So did his mother, who 'bagsied' the clothes after the shoot, although wearing a skirt previously worn by your son is not something every mother can claim to have experienced.

'I loved playing a woman actually,' Kay tells McGuinness on the DVD. 'And I didn't play it in a woman's voice … Andrew Gillman the director told me not to, and it works.' In pre-publicity for the show Peter told the *Independent* on 10 November 1998: 'I've always been able to write female characters – I find women funnier than men, and I love the rhythm of women's speech. I go to Slimmers' World, where it's mostly women, and I get so much material – they have no taboos about what they'll discuss.' Coming from a matriarchal Irish Catholic family, Peter Kay found adopting a female voice far easier than that of a man's.

Father Ted, *Coogan's Run* and *The IT Group* writer and

admirer of Peter Kay, Graham Linehan, agrees and likens some of his stand-up to an Irish comedian he once saw – 'the name escapes me I'm afraid' – who would perform all his gigs with his mother and all her friends on the front row and 'would more or less play to them. The rest of the audience were just along for the ride. I think Peter Kay is very feminine as well,' he added. 'If you notice, a lot of his reference points are from not the usual male references of *Star Wars* and things. His references will be *Dirty Dancing* and, for want of a better word, chick flicks. I think that comes from being close to women and understanding women a bit more. It also tends to take some of the nasty edge off your comedy when you show the female side of yourself. I think that's a real secret to him. If he was from a household full of boys his humour would have been more edgy and defensive, because he'd be coming from a more combative direction, but he's warm and welcoming and that appeals to a lot more people. I'm so sorry for sounding so pretentious!'

Indeed, Peter's acceptance of his X chromosomes stretches to his music taste, which incorporates a love of musicals like *The Kids from Fame* and housewives' pin-up Michael Bublé. 'He's got a special kind of magic, that guy,' he told Radio One's Edith Bowman recently.

Even before 'The Services' aired, Channel 4 had decided to give Peter Kay his own series. Comedian Billy Bedlam remembers appearing on the bill at the Frog and Bucket with him shortly after *The Sunday Show* in 1997, and Peter telling him about a TV series he had planned that was inspired by the 1995 series Graham Linehan had helped write, *Coogan's Run*. 'We chatted backstage and I remember him telling me all about this idea,' says Billy. 'As he was explaining it to me he kept on saying it was like the Steve Coogan series where he played Paul Calf and lots of different characters.'

In early November Peter and his manager Lisa White travelled down to London to meet Channel 4 chief executive Kevin Lygo. The recently appointed Lygo and comedy commissioning editor Katie Taylor had some ideas on how they would like him to develop, but Peter shocked them by outlining in great detail six episodes of a series that continued with the format of 'The Services' with all of the shows set in his native Bolton. They were stunned. He worried that the London-centric TV company might find the last part of his idea hard to swallow, but fortunately it worked in his favour and became one of the deciding factors in the commission. Then governed by guidelines to provide set amounts of hours of different types of shows for as broad a range of viewers as possible, Peter's idea fell into their remit for 'regional programming'. Hurrah! Job's a good 'un, as Bez used to say.

When he spoke to Simon Fanshawe of *The Sunday Times* shortly after the meeting with Lygo he told him he had the green light for the series but 'now it just needs the green, green light ... apparently ... whatever that is'. 'There was some opposition,' Katie Taylor admits. 'We had to fight to get it through.' A couple of weeks after the meeting with Kevin Lygo the 'green, green light' flickered and Peter Kay was signed up to write and perform in six episodes of an as yet untitled series, again to be produced by Sandie Kirk with filming dates scheduled for spring 1999.

'You ... you what? Lancashire against Yorkshire? Bloody hell, Jerry, you don't mix the counties ... Ike and Tina, Chalk and Cheese. They don't go. You're asking for trouble.'

Brian Potter, Phoenix Nights

In the winter of 1998 Peter Kay was to perform to the biggest audiences of his career to date, but first there were smaller, less glamorous local gigs to attend to. One of them was co-compèring an event at the Frog and Bucket club during the Manchester Comedy Festival entitled Raw of the Roses – owner Dave Perkin having come up with an idea to stage a Lancashire versus Yorkshire open-mic comedy duel. It was an evening ripe for disagreement. As Charles Nevin describes the difference between the counties in *Lancashire, Where Women Die of Love*: 'The Pennines are a boundary far more significant than the Trent. On the one side lives a warm and whimsical race, ever ready to chuckle, even laugh, in the face of the sheer ridiculousness of life; on the other, a sad and surly people, unable to understand why they haven't been let in on the joke.'

'My dad used to say people from Lancashire wake up funny,' says Eric Morecambe's son Gary. 'They have the ability to see the world slightly askew, they don't actually see it the same way we do. He wasn't thinking what he was going to have for breakfast, he was just thinking funny, what funny things were going to come his way today. It's completely unique to the north west. And I can definitely see that in Peter Kay, that Lancashire way of looking at things. They look at life differently to everyone else.'

On the Yorkshire team for the Raw of the Roses battle, compèred by Roger Monkhouse, was one man who would later become friends with Peter, Toby Foster from Barnsley. Foster's best material was when he was being heckled by the partisan crowd. When a wag shouted 'Hey fatty', he replied: 'Why do they always pick on comedians? No one ever shouted that at Elvis, did they?' And then he asked, 'Any other Yorkshiremen in?' When a handful responded he told them, 'Great! Enough for a strike. I'll keep them looking this way while you go through the till.'

'I'd never seen Peter before, and he was absolutely fantastic,' says Toby Foster today. 'He blew the room away.' A month later Toby booked him for the comedy night he compèred in the function room above the Fleece and Firkin pub in Barnsley (it's not there any more, sadly). It wasn't very well attended, but Peter Kay fan Steve Alcock, who is now the editor of the blog <stevestate.blogspot.com>, has fond memories of the evening. There were only about 17 people in the room, all on chairs round tables, and Steve and the only friend he'd managed to persuade to shell out the £7 entrance, Neeki, blagged a table down the front. Not letting the small throng bother him, Peter launched into his normal routine – his mum dancing at weddings, people's conversations on buses – when midway through his act Neeki's mobile phone rang. 'She went bright red but didn't switch it off,' says Steve Alcock. 'She answered it and started to whisper into it that she was at a comedy gig. I was so embarrassed, especially when Peter Kay snatched the phone from her and started talking to Neeki's boyfriend, who was calling her. "Could you call back later," he said. "Only we're a bit busy. Ta ra." '

Still, it was better than the previous time he'd played in the Yorkshire citadel. 'Some of the places I've played,' he said. 'In Barnsley once there was a f***in' horse in the room – he got stuck in the doorway.'

After Edinburgh and 'The Services', playing in Barnsley was something of a comedown, but since his Perrier nomination he had appeared at Her Majesty's Theatre in London and the High Hall at Birmingham University. Then came the call that every alternative comedian dreads and every mainstream comedian dreams of, an invitation to appear in the Royal Variety Performance. It used to be called the Royal Variety Command Performance but, as befitted a family lurching from one embarrassment to the next, they no longer had the right to command anyone, let alone the showbiz elite of Great Britain.

'I got a letter asking me if I wanted to do it. I knew it were real because it said I weren't getting paid!' laughs Peter, who nevertheless accepted the call.

Before Peter got himself togged up in a dinner jacket and bow tie for his appointment with royalty he was booked to entertain an entirely different set of queens. On Sunday, 28 October Peter was among the acts booked to perform at the Royal Albert Hall as part of the annual Equality Show, which raised funds for Stonewall, the pressure group lobbying for gay and lesbian equal rights. The show was directed by famous Bolton old boy Sir Ian McKellen and presented by Rhona Cameron and Graham Norton.

Peter had run into Graham Norton a year previously when they shared the bill in Manchester. Norton was headlining, and in the dressing room before the show he asked Peter: 'What's the name of the gay area in Manchester?' Rather than tell Norton it was the area around Canal Street, he replied, straight-faced, 'The gay area of Manchester is Bury.' At the end of his set Graham Norton told his audience, 'I've got to go now, ladies and gentlemen.' And seeking to seal his approval with the gay members of the crowd, he added: 'I've got to get down to Bury.' Silence.

With no concessions to the audience, Peter held the Royal Albert Hall crowd in the palm of his hand. For a comic performing for the first time at such a large venue it was little short of miraculous. 'Before he went on I gave him one piece of advice,' says his manager, Lisa White. 'The Royal Albert Hall is massive and the acoustics for a comedian are not great, so I told him to wait for the laugh. It takes a while for the laugh to get to the back. And he did. And he absolutely stormed it.'

Just as at small comedy clubs, his forensic observations of life, TV and childhood reminded the audience of things they'd forgotten they knew. Like the fact that 'there's always a full gateau left at the end of weddings', or when you need to use up a roll of film from your holiday you take a picture of the dog in front of the fire or your mum on the patio. If you were looking for proof that Peter Kay could appeal to everyone, this was the night. Peter didn't get the biggest laugh of the evening, though. That came when *EastEnders* 'songbird' Martine McCutcheon attempted to reach out to her gay audience by murdering Diana Ross's 'I'm Coming Out'. 'I'm coming out, I want the world to know ...' sang the actress formerly known as Tiffany. 'Yeah, you wish,' came the heckle back. McCutcheon was booked to play the 77th Royal Variety Performance too, at the Lyceum Ballroom a month later, but instead of bawling out a camp anthem she joined Barry Manilow, Boyzone's Ronan Keating and Stephen Gately to croon Frank Sinatra's 'They Can't Take That Away from Me'. It was not the finest of cover versions although Manilow and McCutcheon made an amusingly mismatched couple – like a Concorde parked next to Budgie the Little Helicopter.

Peter Kay toned down his act too, but suffered one of the most embarrassing moments of his career during rehearsals: 'You do a quick run-through of your act and there were people hammering nails in behind me and Barry Manilow stood in front of me,' he says. 'I had a small tape player which I played songs through as part of my act, but the radio mic I was using caused the tape to speed up so everyone sounded like Pinky and Perky. But everyone in the audience was roaring with laughter, including Barry Manilow. I was saying: "This isn't my act!" They were saying: "But it's funny. Can't you make do?" I said: "I can't make do, the Queen's coming!" So they sent out for another dictaphone and I got five back in the end. That really frightened me. But in the end it was fine.'

In fact Peter needn't have worried about the Queen catching him off guard. She'd decided to stay at home and watch *The Vicar of Dibley* with a few cans of Stella and a thin-crust pepperoni instead (well, possibly), leaving the duty of mixing it with showbiz hoi polloi to the Prince of Wales. As Paul O'Grady in his Lily Savage guise remarked in the direction of the royal box during the show, 'I bet when that envelope comes through the front door you all draw straws for who comes to this.'

Peter's mother, Deirdre, and nan, Edith, were in the audience though for his big occasion. The £100 tickets were a gift in return for constantly answering the phone from people offering him work. Eventually Peter would buy an answering machine for his business calls, the contraption telling callers, 'Hello, you've reached Peter. If it's about showbiz call my agent. Ta ra.' Sadly the Royal Variety Performance wasn't Peter's finest 10 minutes on a London stage. As Charlie Catchpole wrote in the *Mirror*: 'Typically, the most original act on the bill – the brilliant comic from Bolton, Peter Kay – died a death. His revelations that "Turn, Turn, Turn" by the Byrds is really the theme from *Crossroads* and that Celine Dion actually sings "I believe that the hot dogs go on" went over the audience's head like a Cruise missile.' Instead it was cruise ship entertainer Jane McDonald and rubber-faced impressionist Phil Cool who pleased the attending Prime Minister Tony Blair and Prince Charles the most. Maybe Peter should have stuck with Pinky and Perky after all.

This year, 1998, was the one when the Spice Girls grabbed all the headlines at the event. Not because of their singing, but because in the traditional meet and greet after the show the Prince broke with centuries of royal protocol and lightly touched the pregnant Victoria Beckham's bump. This invasion was possibly in return for having his arse pinched by the Girls when they last met. Two places along, as Charlie boy was getting all zig-a-zig-ah with Posh Spice, Paul O'Grady and Peter gurned mock 'Carry On' looks of surprise.

The next day Peter was due to attend a gala luncheon – ham and egg pie, Quavers, all good stuff – with some of the cast, but didn't make it because he was due back in Manchester at the Levenshulme Palace to play a benefit gig for victims of the Omagh bombing. 'He has not let the fame and fortunes of his two-year meteoric rise to fame go to his head,' Palace owner Lawrence Hennigan told the *Bolton Evening News*, as if he were reading from an autocue. 'All he wanted was a plateful of scampi and chips and a pint of Pepsi Cola.'

A few days after this slight return to his 'will perform for food' early years he was back in London at LWT's South Bank studios for the 1998 British Comedy Awards. The comedy elite were all there – Steve Coogan, whose *I'm Alan Partridge* was the comedy hit of the year, Harry Enfield, Dawn French and Paul Merton. The organisers had hit upon the idea of it being a fancy-dress event and for everyone to turn up in a Latin theme. But being a cynical bunch, every single one of the comedians attending the event dressed in their normal suits and ties – apart from *Jonathan Creek* actor and stand-up comic Alan Davies, who sheepishly sat at a table dressed as a matador. As the evening progressed and the guests got increasingly drunk a new game began called 'Throw Things at Alan Davies' and bread rolls hurtled through the air as Jonathan Ross attempted to keep order. Not that Peter joined in. He was too busy feeling awestruck by being in the same room as Victoria Wood.

Peter had been nominated in several categories, both as Top Television Newcomer and Top Stand-Up Comedian, but in the event lost out to Irishmen Dylan Moran and his Perrier Award conqueror in Edinburgh, Tommy Tiernan, respectively. He didn't win, but in the eye of the discerning comedy connoisseurs the nominations still ranked as another promotion.

Peter found himself in demand with the media and in one extraordinary interview with the *Scotsman* he took the journalist on a tour of Bolton's finest shopping precincts (principally because he had to visit Susan in Boots and take a couple of videos back to the library and didn't see any reason to change his plans for the visiting gentleman of the press). Such a matter-of-fact approach to publicity took the visiting journalist by surprise. 'Peter Kay doesn't want to meet you in London, at the Groucho Club or some such see-and-be-seen watering-hole just so you can appreciate what an accomplished air-kisser he is,' wrote Aidan Smith. 'You have to go to Bolton.' Bolton? he must have wondered. Don't people become famous so they can leave places like Bolton? Peter continued to give the journalist a tour of the sights pointing out the market and the town's Christmas lights: 'A pig switched them on last week, Bolton's very own Babe. It's got foot-and-mouth apparently.'

Ah, Bolton, land of dreams, a town of dreaming spires and campaniles, college squares and willow trees. No, hang on, that's Oxford. Bolton's a bit more down-to-earth than all that, a town built on hard graft and fed on pies and gravy with a proper Victorian town hall looming over the lot of it and casting the bulk of the town centre in perpetual shadow. It's a glorious sight. Beyond the town centre Bolton today is made up of half a dozen other towns – Kearsley, Farnworth, Horwich, Blackrod, Little Lever and Westhoughton – and when you add it all up it makes Bolton the second biggest town in England (Northampton claims first prize) – although Wigan also boasts of the same thing, which feeds the healthy rivalry between the two neighbours. In fact the bulk of Dave Spikey's live set centres around Wigan jokes. Bolton's people were voted the friendliest in Britain, according to a survey carried out by the British Society for the Advancement of Science. It is home to the world's largest manufacturer of disposable bedpans, a national school for training the blind, the most zealous traffic wardens in the world (just try spending 30 seconds longer than it says on your parking ticket!) and thanks to good town planning, no tower blocks and a far lower mugger-to-pensioner ratio than most places in England. Cunningly, it is surrounded by a complex ring of motorways and one-way A roads, making it rather like Las Vegas casinos in that it's easy to go into but virtually impossible to leave. In common with the rest of the country, most Mancunians have never set foot in Peter Kay's home town and regard Boltonians as a different species who talk oddly, like the old joke: 'A bald cat gets on a bus in Bolton without paying and the driver asks, "Where's your fur?"' Southerners may like to imagine that avocados and lapsang souchong have yet to make it this far north, but Bolton's booming. There are hundreds of wealthy Asian entrepreneurs, hotels spring up everywhere and a gleaming new football stadium. Oddly, however, it seems to have retained a 1950s identity that other towns and cities have long since lost.

Of course Peter Kay's a Boltonian, he couldn't come from anywhere else – his humour suits his accent (or is it the other way round?), he's canny, daft and no-nonsense. He's fortunate enough to come from a town where people still talk to each other in shops, but unfortunate to live in a place where pastry is included on the list of a day's crucial vitamins and minerals.

Bolton was once famous for its football team, Bolton Wanderers, and their valiant captain Nat Lofthouse, who scored a goal in the 1958 FA Cup Final by pushing Manchester United's goalkeeper Harry Gregg and the ball he was holding into the back of the net, and also for the soot and grime produced by the town's multitude of mill chimneys. Then it became even more famous for the man who helped pull them all down, steeplejack Fred Dibnah, who enjoyed celebrity after nearly being crushed by a falling stack during a BBC news report. As much as his hair-raising demolition jobs, it was Dibnah's rough-hewn manner, permanent flat cap and pearls of Lancastrian wisdom that made him a star. 'A man who says he feels no fear,' he said, 'is either a fool or a liar.'

As well as Dibnah (RIP), Bolton is the birthplace of no fewer than three former Radio One DJs: Sara Cox, Vernon Kay and Mark Radcliffe; Badly Drawn Boy man Damon Gough; children's TV presenter Johnny Ball, pop art painter Patrick Caulfield; *Crackerjack*'s Stu 'I could crush a grape' Francis; actor Frank Findlay; film critic Leslie Halliwell; and teenage female arm-wrestling champion Dawn Higson (arm currently insured for £40,000). Despite such stiff competition even before Peter Kay had turned it into a TV location, he was Bolton's favourite son. Such was the local newspaper's obsession with him that in December 1998 they even ran photos of a Peter Kay look-alike who couldn't have looked less like Peter Kay if he'd been wearing a balaclava – unless the look-alike bit was confined to his waist measurement. Even so, Bolton loved Peter Kay and Peter Kay loved Bolton right back. It wasn't just the fact that he felt at home there, that he could 'go to the chippy in my slippers (you can't do that down London, you'd get arrested!)', it was special.

'I love Bolton. I really, really love it,' he has said. 'You could do a Woody Allen in Bolton, do 40 films and still find something new because there's something new in every house.' Over the forthcoming three years he'd be doing just that.

For Peter, Bolton was home, inspiration and shortly location for his new series. Unlike the other acts who had recently emerged from the north-west area – Steve Coogan, *The Royle Family* cast of Caroline Aherne, Craig Cash and Ralf Little, *The Fast Show*'s John Thomson, Paul 'Lily

Savage' O'Grady – he saw no reason to leave his birthplace and relocate to London.

'Bolton is home, and it's normal,' he says. 'People never treat me any different and I like that. I'm not anti-London, but I just think, "Why do we have to go to London?" I love being at home. Life is all about your family and friends. I'd rather pack it all in than go and live there. I can go down to London and perform at some flash corporate do, and the next day I'm in my tracksuit bottoms eating me mam's cooking. And it seems to me like the only real bit was Bolton – the rest of it never happened.'

Fortune if not fame seemed to hold little appeal for Peter Kay in 1998 and, when pressed on where his ambitions lay, he replied frankly that all he wanted was to 'get married and buy a house and settle down. And they would be, like, the most important things in my life. So it wouldn't matter what other people thought, as long as I could find some way to keep on writing, or whatever, even if it was some chat show on cable.'

Ending his article for the *Scotsman*, Aidan Smith concluded, 'Make no mistake, Peter Kay is going places. Today Bolton, tomorrow Bolton, too.'

The words Peter gave to Pearl in 'The Services' as she drives in for another day's work seemed to apply to him and his feelings for his home town. 'I must have driven down here a million times,' she says, glancing flirtatiously into camera. 'Still brings the hairs up on the back of me neck, though. You know, they say home is where the heart is. Well, my heart definitely belongs here, in First Services Bolton. She's my first, my last, my everything.'

The way that Peter Kay has rooted his entire career in his home town is incredible. He has said, 'You write about what you know, and what I know is Bolton.' But there must be more to it than this. In trying to quantify what it is that makes him funny, the answer is always 'Bolton' – the people, his memories, his family (his father's side go back centuries in the town). It is almost as if he feels that if he leaves the place of his birth some magic and luck will disappear.

The other thing that roots him to the town is his mother. He was always a mother's boy, but the bond grew when his father left home. Leaving Bolton would feel like desertion, so when he is in the business of househunting for himself and for her his major criterion is that they shouldn't be more than two songs away from each other on the car radio.

Like all sons who are particularly close to their mothers, the need for approval is never far away, and it's not just laughs Peter is looking for when he passes his scripts on to his mum, it's endorsement.

Carry on caravanning: A teenage Peter with teacher John Clough and friend Michael Atherton in Bouth, Cumbria.

It's spitting: Peter aged 17, in the Lake District, with school friend Michael Atherton.

Roar potential: Peter the Cowardly Lion relaxes backstage during the school's performance of *The Wizard of Oz*.

Bowled over: At home the day after winning the *City Life* 'North West Comedian of the Year' competition in 1996.